Indoor Gardens and Window-boxes

Indoor Gardens
and
Window-boxes

Gisela Gramenz

Lutterworth Press
London

ISBN 0 7188 1783 4
First published in Great Britain 1971
Translated from the German
"Grünes und Blüten für Fenster und Balkon"
by Margaret Baker

Copyright © 1969 Otto Maier Verlag
Ravensburg, Germany

English translation copyright © 1971
Lutterworth Press, London
Printed in Great Britain by
Ebenezer Baylis and Son, Limited,
The Trinity Press, Worcester, and London

Contents

What Do Plants Need?

A plant is only beautiful when it is flourishing and doing well. In its natural habitat every plant finds what it needs, but plants indoors are like animals in a cage—they are dependent on our care if they are to thrive. They exist under unnatural conditions and so it is important to provide them with conditions that are as natural as possible: for instance, to choose plants for the house according to the conditions that we can offer. To maintain life every plant needs light, air, water, warmth and food and, of course, it needs them in specific and exactly balanced proportions which differ for each kind of plant. The Law of the Minimum which Justus von Liebig discovered in the last century applies here: it says that a plant can develop only according to the growth factor of which the smallest amount is available. Extra warmth or water cannot make up for a lack of light; in fact, too much of one thing can actually be harmful, when something else is lacking.

Care is necessary, but you can have too much of a good thing—as Paracelsus says, "Anything can be a poison, and only the amount will decide whether it is a poison or not!"

Varying degrees of adaptability

The essential requirements of individual types of plant are very different, depending on the natural conditions of their original habitats. There are some kinds of plant which display an amazing adaptability and which also continue to grow happily even when their optimum requirements are exceeded or under-estimated; others again are very sensitive and, if their needs are not properly met, react obstinately with stunted growth and diseases.

Acclimatization also plays a decided part: plants which have been grown in a nurseryman's greenhouse, or which have been "forced" by professional tricks, often react badly to the change to what, for them, is an unfavourable environment, while examples of the same species which have been brought into the unfavourable habitat as young plants, or which have been raised there as cuttings, come to maturity without difficulty.

Anyone who wants to cultivate plants successfully in the house or on a balcony (without too much work) must first of all be clear as to what the plant needs, what living conditions can be provided in the house, and how much time, energy and money can be devoted to this hobby.

The poinsettia belongs to the short-day plants which form buds only when they receive less than twelve hours of light a day.

By shutting off the light or providing additional lighting from lamps, the professional gardener can alter the bud development of many plants—for instance, chrysanthemums: as short-day plants they only form buds when there is less than twelve hours' light a day, but they can come into flower in the summer.

Light and Sun

Plants need light for photosynthesis: during this process, which is also called assimilation, the plant takes carbonic acid out of the air, removes the oxygen and converts the carbon it contains into carbon compounds which are used for the development and nourishment of the plant. This process takes place in the cells which contain chlorophyll, the green substance in leaves (but even plants with coloured leaves—white, yellow or red—contain traces of chlorophyll).

The amount of light which plants require for assimilation varies widely. The scale ranges from the plants of the steppe and desert which need full sunlight to the ferns and mosses which thrive in the twilight beneath heavy tree cover or in caves. Every species has its own particular requirements and if these are persistently over- or under-catered for, growth will suffer.

Short-day and long-day plants

The rhythm of the change from night to day and of the variation in the length of day from summer to winter also plays a part in the development of the plant. The periods of growth, rest, and of flower and fruit formation are controlled by this. Gardeners refer to short-day and long-day plants. The former develop their flower buds when the day is less than twelve hours long, while the latter (and most summer flowers belong to this group) only bloom properly when they are in the light for fourteen hours or more each day.

Decrease of light in a room

This dependence on light means that you cannot place plants just where you like in the house, at least not for any length of time. They must receive a minimum quantity of light, depending on the conditions obtaining in their natural habitat. For most plants this means a place near the window. Only a few shade-loving plants, primarily natives of the primeval forest, do well with the light that reaches the depth of the room, and even then the room must be very well lit.

We are moreover usually inclined to overestimate the amount of light inside a closed-in room. Even a plant which stands right in front of a window receives only about half as much light as a plant in the open, for it gets the light only on one side, while in the open rays of light reach the plant from above and from all round.

Add to this the rapid decrease of light in a room. The amount of light decreases as the square of the distance from the window, and it is therefore normal that only one five-hundredth of the amount of light measured at the window reaches the farthest corner of the room.

If you want to place plants in such an unfavourable spot, you must either keep a second specimen of the same type in a more favourable place as a reserve and switch the two at frequent intervals, or you must make use of artificial lighting.

Extra light from lamps

Additional lighting has long been used in the professional cultivation of ornamental plants in order to accelerate growth or prolong blooming. From this it has emerged that several hours of artificial lighting daily is very beneficial to plants and contributes to their healthy growth.

This is a particularly good way of helping plants during the dark winter months. The most suitable method of providing additional lighting in a living room is to use warm-toned fluorescent tubes which should be mounted about two feet (60 cm) above the plants. They give a pleasant natural light. Lamps with normal filaments give too much warmth and are therefore not suitable. Lighting of this kind is not only useful but decorative too. A "room garden", with indirect lighting, can be very effective.

Sunlight can be dangerous

However important it is, on the one hand, to provide suffi-cient light for plants in the house, direct sunlight is, on the other hand, very dangerous. This is the reason for the so-called glasshouse effect. When the sun's rays meet a solid object (such as leaves, soil, flower pots) heat builds up. Out in the open this heat is taken up by the surrounding air and dispersed by the natural circulation of the air.

On a window sill, however, the glass pane reflects the heat rays and sometimes the air between the plant and the window reaches a temperature of 120°–140°F (50°–60°C) and more because of the intensity of the sun's rays and the lack of fresh air. This heat bath is too much even for cacti accustomed to desert conditions. The plants are scorched.

It is not just the direction in which your window faces, but also the immediate neighbourhood that is important. Narrow streets and tall trees absorb a good deal of light, while a north-facing window, with a view over open country, can be very light indeed, even without sun, for sky and clouds reflect the light.

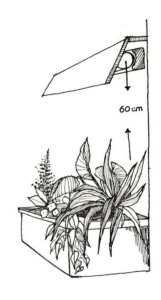

You can help plants through the dark winter months by providing artificial lighting. For this the normal ceiling lights of your room are not sufficient. The best plan is to use fluorescent tubes which are shielded at the side, posi-tioned about 2½–3 ft above your plants. A special gadget which switches the lamps on automatically when the day-light fades will make life simpler!

If your plants are standing in a window which receives several hours of direct sunlight each day, then you will need some means of providing shade. The best solution is a blind or awning fitted on the outside of the window.

For plants which have to stand in a south-facing window you should always provide some form of shade (awning, or blind), preferably outside the window. Otherwise you must remove the plants when the sun is shining or temporarily cover them with paper. You can only do without shades for east and west-facing windows if you have good ventilation and choose the appropriate sun-loving plants.

Phototropism

Plants show that they are starved of light chiefly by phototropism. They turn their leaves and shoots towards the light and so show their reverse and less attractive side to the room. The attempt to persuade the plant to grow straight, as it would in the open or in a greenhouse lit on all sides, by turning the pot frequently, usually ends in interrupted growth and the loss of leaves and buds. You must put up with lop-sided growth or fix up some additional lighting on the other side.

Temperatures

In addition to light, one factor whose importance for the success of plants is usually undervalued or completely overlooked, is the correct temperature. One is all too easily inclined to believe that living conditions which human beings find comfortable must also be suitable for house plants. However, many, if not the majority of the failures in house-plant cultivation, result from the discrepancy between the needs of people and plants.

These failures are less obvious in summer when the plants do well during extended daylight and higher temperatures than in the winter during the short days. Then most plants pass through a kind of rest period during which all the vital functions are reduced and their need for warmth is less.

Three climatic zones

House plants can be divided into three groups, depending on their origin and the climatic conditions of their natural habitats:

1. Plants from temperate to Mediterranean zones which in winter need temperatures of 45°–50°F, at most 53° (8°–10°, at most 12°C), pass through a definite rest period during which no new leaves are formed; however many set their buds at this time.
2. Plants from sub-tropical zones which, during the period of minimum light in winter, prefer temperatures of 60°–65°F (14°–18°C) and cannot withstand temperatures lower than 50°F (12°C).
3. Plants from the tropics which, even in winter, always need temperatures of at least 65°F (18°C) and more.

The nurseryman counts the first group as cold house plants, the second belongs to the temperate or intermediate house, and the third is grown in the hot house at temperatures from 65°–77°F (18°–25°C).

Only plants in the last group can readily stand the high temperatures which normally prevail in winter in our heated living rooms, provided, of course, that they receive sufficient light.

The plants of the second group too do well in a living room if they have a very light position which is not in the immediate neighbourhood of the heat source. In homes heated by

Many plants require cooler temperatures in winter during their resting period. This is why the rubber plant (Ficus elastica) has become one of our most popular house plants; it can stand the warmth of a normally heated room very well.

Plants from cooler zones withstand high winter temperatures better if they are given extra light.

The myrtle needs a temperature of about 45°F (8°C) in winter. You can only keep it in light, unheated rooms.

The Christmas cactus—like all flowering plants—suffers from heat stroke if it is transferred in winter from the greenhouse to a well-heated room. You must place it in a cooler spot first.

a fire or stove the temperature near the window usually meets their needs, all the more so as the temperature in such rooms as a rule goes down during the night. In modern centrally-heated houses, however, there is often a radiator under the window, in which case this pot would be too warm.

If plants are placed in the immediate vicinity of hot rising air from a radiator (often 86°F [30°C]), they suffer leaf scorch. You must therefore take precautions (widening and insulating the window sill, the establishment of a plant trough etc; see page 31); so that the plants are not affected directly at least by the warm air from the radiator. If possible, the radiator should be switched off at night.

Plants of the first group can only be kept for a long period if they stand in an unheated room (bedroom, landing, hall) or between the panes of a double-glazed window.

Slow acclimatization

It is important to realize that pot plants which come fresh from the nursery or flower shop need a slow acclimatization to the temperature of your room. Flowering plants in particular will otherwise suffer a severe shock. Even if at first sight it seems discourteous, place a cyclamen or azalea which someone has given you in full bloom, as a winter present, not in the usually overheated living room but in a cooler place, for a couple of hours at least. If you don't, the flowers and leaves will droop within a few hours and will not recover, but if it is acclimatized slowly, you will enjoy its blooms for weeks.

A cold draught is just as dangerous to house plants in winter as too much heat, and particularly when it is a constant draught which comes through badly fitting doors and windows, like a sudden cold front in the atmosphere. If there is no chance of moving the plants, then you must cover them for the time being with paper.

On very cold days (and, of course, nights) you may find that leaves and flowers which are too close to the window pane freeze. You can stretch a sheet of transparent plastic across the inside of the window frame as a protection against cold, but it is better to provide some form of heating (see page 34).

Plants suffer from "cold feet" too

The temperature round the roots as well as the general temperature of the room plays a part in the well-being of a plant. It should be at least as high as the temperature of the room and it ought to be 4°–5°F (2°–3°C) above it. If it is significantly higher, or when it sinks considerably below the room temperature, then root damage may occur.

The first case occurs comparatively seldom, only when the pot stands directly on a heat source or when it is made of a dark substance and absorbs heat from the sun (metal outer containers heat up very quickly!). On the other hand, more frequently than is generally realized, cooling of the roots is responsible for stunted growth. It can be caused by draughts (badly fitting window frames), by the cold caused by evaporation on the outside of a clay pot (see page 27) and by insufficient insulation of plant troughs which have been let into the outside wall (see page 34).

Warm air requires greater humidity

The problem of humidity is closely linked with the plant's ability to withstand heat. Of course, there is a range of plants from dry, desert areas which can stand a very dry room atmosphere. But, in order to thrive, most need a minimum humidity of 50–60% and some sensitive inhabitants of tropical and sub-tropical rain forests require at least 75%.

In summer this percentage is usually achieved, but it is a different matter in winter: in a normally heated room, without the help of a humidifier, it is often only 30%. High winds reduce this percentage even further. The cold air which comes in is certainly saturated with moisture, but, when it is warmed, it absorbs further moisture from the room. Humidity is therefore a relative value: the warmer the air is, the more water vapour it can take up without becoming saturated and without releasing minute water droplets (you can easily observe this phenomenon in reverse: when the air in a warm damp room is suddenly cooled, everything is covered with a film of water).

During this process additional water is removed from plants too. You yourself find the dry air uncomfortable—but your reaction is probably to fling the window open again to let in "fresh" air, and the cycle begins all over again.

Effective humidifiers

Only an effective installation for humidifying the air can help. The usual ceramic containers, which hang on the stove or radiator, are barely adequate, particularly when they are

Falls in temperature and—above all—draughts are the invisible enemies of house plants. Windows which do not shut properly should definitely be draught-proofed in winter!

Begonia rex withstands heated rooms very well, provided the air is not too dry and it has a light (but not sunny) position.

Humidity makes the climate of heated rooms pleasanter for people as well as plants. Pottery water containers hanging on the radiators are not adequate.

The bright-leaved croton belongs to a beautiful but delicate group of plants. It certainly needs high temperatures, but at the same time it requires such a degree of humidity that you can only really keep it for a long period in an enclosed window garden with a humidifier.

made of glazed pottery for aesthetic reasons and in practice present only a limited surface area from which evaporation can take place.

The following methods are more effective: shallow bowls placed on the stove or radiator, plastic sponges in perforated plastic containers or gadgets in which the warm air from the heating is passed through a kind of blotting paper which soaks up water from a metal container. In a normal room of 65 cubic yards' capacity (50 cubic metres), you can use up to 4 pints (2 litres) of water daily in this way.

Finally there are various electric humidifiers which you can link, if you wish, with a hygrometer which measures humidity and which automatically maintains a constant humidity. The plants themselves can help to improve the atmosphere of the room when they are arranged in groups and not as single specimens. They can be further sustained by the use of plant troughs (see page 31) filled with peat or pebbles.

Water

The soft green parts of plants are 90% water, and even in the woody parts 50–60% water is present. Water provides for the transport of nutrients from the roots to the outermost tips of the leaves and in the opposite direction carries the starch compounds formed in the leaves (see Assimilation, page 8) back into the stem and the roots. Hydrostatic pressure keeps the soft parts of the plant, in particular the leaves and flowers, upright and rigid ("turgidity" is the botanical name for this process). When water is lacking, the leaves become first of all flabby and limp, and they then dry out.

African hemp or house lime, with its big soft leaves, is particularly sensitive to a lack of water. If the leaves begin to droop, it must be thoroughly watered at once.

How much water do plants need?

The amount of water required by plants varies according to their origin, habitat and stage of development. Young plants and plants which are growing fast or are in full bloom need more water than those which are resting and older, mature plants. The humidity and temperature of air play an important part here: dry heat increases evaporation, cold and damp decrease it.

Unfortunately you cannot always make up for a lack of water simply by supplying it in large quantities. Much depends on the differing constitutions of plants. Plants from areas which are constantly wet, in particular those from the damp warmth of tropical forests, with large quantities of delicate unprotected leaves, are accustomed to a constant supply of water and, at the same time, to a high degree of humidity. In dry air they simply cannot manage to replace the water lost through the leaves by evaporation by taking in a correspondingly large amount of water through the roots. Other plants, on the contrary, which come from areas where the water supply is intermittent, in particular from steppe and desert regions which are completely dry for months at a time, are perfectly adapted to dry conditions. Some of them have fleshy swollen stems or leaves—cacti and succulents for instance—or underground tubers, bulbs and rootstocks (rhizomes) in which they store water during periods of plenty in order to survive during long droughts. In addition they are protected against evaporation by a thick coating of hairs, by a waxy covering or by having tiny leathery leaves.

*You cannot always satisfy higher demands for water by simply using **your** watering-can.*

15

Echeveria, like cacti and other succulents (plants with thick, fleshy leaves), are well used to living in dry conditions. They store water and begin to rot if they are given too much to drink.

Too much water causes more damage than too little; many plants die off because they are literally drowned. Far fewer die from a lack of water.

While you can keep plants of the first group usually only in a greenhouse or an enclosed window garden, the others can adapt completely to the climate in our living rooms. Some even require a definite dry period for their proper development; during this they often, of course, lose their leaves (flowering bulbs originating in steppe regions, such as tulips, hyacinths, and also amaryllis and some kinds of orchid, belong to this group). With others periods of high demand for water alternate with times when, during the rest period, usually in the winter months, the requirement is small.

Rain from a watering-can

In your home the watering-can takes the place of the natural water supply provided by rain and moisture held in the soil. From what we have said earlier it follows that watering should not follow a set pattern. If you use the method or "a shot of water in each flower pot each day" many a plant will be killed with kindness.

It is nearly always better to water infrequently, but very thoroughly, and then to wait until the soil in the flower pot dries out again. The roots in particular need a minimum amount of air as well as water and nutrients. If more water is given than the plant needs, the water content of the pot rises, the soil becomes waterlogged (see page 26) and the roots begin to rot. As they can no longer fulfil their function —taking up water—the same symptoms occur in plants as when they lack water; the leaves become limp, flabby, yellow and brown, and the flowers wither and fall off. Inexperienced plant lovers react to these symptoms by giving more and more water, making the situation even worse. The only solution in such cases is to take the plant out of the pot, to remove the waterlogged earth and all the dead brown or black roots (healthy roots look white or yellowish) and to place the plant in fresh soil. Finally you must cut the plant back a little to match the capacity for taking up water of the reduced root mass. Afterwards you must be very careful about watering until new growth shows that the plant has recovered.

Tapping the pot is unreliable

How can we find out exactly how much water a plant needs? Tapping the pot is often recommended for use in the home. If you tap your knuckle against the pot, a muffled sound shows that sufficient water is still available; on the other hand a ringing sound indicates that the plant needs to be watered. In practice, however, this method proves to be unreliable, for large pots sound differently from small ones, the composition of the soil plays a part too, and with modern plastic pots the method fails altogether.

It is safer to rely on accurate observation: if the surface soil has dried out (if you are uncertain, you can scratch the surface a little with a stick) and if the leaves of the plant are drooping slightly—and only very slightly—then it is time to water.

Soaking

Many plants react well to a good soak at intervals of eight to fourteen days. To do this you place them in a bowl with water up to the rim of the pot and leave them for as long as little air bubbles continue to rise (a maximum of half an hour). Then you allow them to drain thoroughly and re-place them on their saucers or in their containers.

Soaking like this is also the one radical remedy with which you can attempt to save a plant whose soil ball has completely dried out. Many plants, such as primulas, hydrangeas and cyclamens, recover remarkably well and very quickly.

No water in the saucer

In no case should surplus water be allowed to remain standing for a long time in the saucer. A footbath of this kind damages the roots (see above). A simple exception: Umbrella plant *(Cyperus alternifolius)* which, as a marsh plant, loves standing in water all the time.

Should plants be watered from above or below?

With the exception of the bromeliads which as "urn plants" are accustomed to obtain their water through their leaf tubes, no plants like having a stream of water poured right into their hearts. Some, such as cyclamens, gloxinias and African violets, rot if water lies between the leaves and the crown from which the flowers grow. If these plants are growing in very small pots, watering from above is difficult. You can water them by filling the saucer with water, provided that the pot has a hole in its base through which the water can be soaked up. However, with this method too, any water left over must be poured out of the saucer after half an hour so that no moisture remains.

Allow the water to stand first

To avoid chilling the roots, you should always water your

Plants growing in standard potting composts or soil-less composts should not be allowed to dry out completely. They should be kept damper than plants in ordinary potting soil, for these potting media do not become waterlogged so easily.

Only the umbrella plant (Cyperus) appreciates having its feet permanently standing in water.

Soft rain water or melted snow does all house plants good. These days water from rivers, streams and ponds is unfortunately seldom free from pollution and disease organisms. You should not use it for watering your plants.

The camellia, one of our loveliest house plants, is often disappointing because it is not properly watered. It needs absolutely lime-free water and a high degree of humidity and should be given neither too little nor too much water.

The water spray should produce a fine mist of minute droplets.

plants with water at room temperature. The best plan is to refill the can immediately after each watering, so that you always have water which has stood for a time and is of the correct temperature. This has another advantage too: in natural conditions plants receive lime-free soft rainwater. Our tap water, on the other hand, nearly always contains a certain amount of lime and is hard. Constant watering with hard water causes lime residues to collect in the flower pot, and only a very few plants like soils which contain a good deal of lime (see 'Soil reaction', page 25). If you allow the water in the can to stand (for at least 24 hours), a part of these lime residues will collect at the bottom. You do not, of course, use the last drops in the can.

If you have very hard tap water, you must take other measures as well. You can buy from your nurseryman or garden centre water-softening tablets which should be used according to the directions. A small bag of peat, hung for 24 hours in the watering can (2 oz peat to 2 gallons of water: [50 gm dry peat to 10 litres of water]) extracts the lime content from the water. The peat cannot, of course, be used for anything afterwards.

Finally, you can often collect rain water, melt snow or use the water which collects in the drip tray when you defrost your refrigerator.

Spraying and sprinkling

Plants which take up a great deal of water have a happier life as room plants if you spray them regularly. For this you need an atomizer which really reduces the water to a very fine mist (you can find these plastic sprays at a garden centre.) Ideally you also need lime-free water, for hard water produces unpleasant spots on the leaves.

Flower sprays which distribute the water in thick streams and drops are only good for occasionally cleaning dust off the leaves. For the same purpose you can, at more infrequent intervals, put the plants in the bath and gently rinse them with the shower, if it is too much bother to wipe the leaves, one at a time, with a damp sponge (use plain water only, not soapy!). Even better and more refreshing is a warm, gentle summer rain.

Of course, it is only plants with strong hardy leaves which can stand such a shower bath. Plants with tender or hairy leaves (such as the African violet) should, if necessary, be dusted dry with a fine brush.

Soils and Plant Foods

In natural conditions plants sink their roots into the soil to take hold in it and to draw from it water and nourishment. According to the locality, this soil consists of mineral constituents in grains of varying size and in different combinations (the various rocks, sand, chalk, clay and loam) and of humus (organic constituents of animal or vegetable origin which have decayed in the soil, i.e. they have decomposed). The amount of humus substances determines the fertility of a soil, for they ensure that the soil is soft, porous, crumbly, moisture-retaining and yet at the same time well aerated. In addition the acidity resulting from decomposition helps the plant's roots to take up the mineral substances which are found in the soil or which are artificially added to it. The humus in the soil must be continually replenished—in natural conditions this happens automatically, through dying vegetation, leaf fall in autumn and so on; humus must be added through intensive feeding of the soil in agriculture and even more so in horticulture. The farmer does it with dung and green manure, the gardener with compost, leaf mould, peat and other organic substances (among these are the various manures, hoof and horn meal, bone meal and dried blood).

Gardeners have special recipes

It is obvious that plants which have to live in flower pots with much less room than in open ground need particularly good soil which will give them the nourishment they need in its best form. A few years ago every gardener had his own more or less secret recipe from which he mixed a potting compost to give each plant, as far as possible, its appropriate mixture of soils. Even today you can still find in many gardening books instructions like this: "Take two parts of sharp sand, one part of well-seasoned farmyard manure, one part of beech leaf mould, one part of good loam, one part of peat and a handful of hoof and horn . . ." Fortunately for all those whose gardening is restricted to the balcony and the house and who have little opportunity of assembling all the ingredients needed, let alone the space needed to allow beech leaves, compost, manure and the other raw materials to stand for a sufficiently long time, research has made great

Dracaena is one of the hardiest and most rewarding house plants.

19

Grandma's pet recipe for potting soil of "Two spadefuls of horse manure to one bucket of garden soil" is outdated. There is no need to go hunting through woods and pastures; you can use ready-made potting composts instead.

Of course, you must make sure that you obtain this soil either from a reliable nursery or, if you buy it in plastic bags, that the name, manufacturer and details of the ingredients are fully listed. Much that is sold privately as "first-class potting soil" does not live up to its expectations, and unfortunately the first you know about it is when your plants fail, and by then it is too late.

strides in recent years. Most gardeners today no longer bother to mix their own special composts in such a complicated manner. They use standardized composts and other industrially prepared soil mixtures which are specially conceived to meet the needs of pot plants and are suitable for nearly all plants, with a few exceptions such as azaleas, heathers and other heaths, bromeliads, orchids, cacti and other succulents. But even for these plants special mixtures can be bought.

A standard compost is nearly always correct

Anyone who wishes to supply house or balcony plants with fresh earth will do well to keep to these ready-made composts. The quantities needed are not so large that price need be considered too seriously. The extra cost is worthwhile for you know that you are actually getting a soil mixture which is suitable for your plants and which, in contrast to garden compost or even plain soil, is rich in nutrients and humus and contains a reserve of fertilizer. Ready-made mixtures are also free from disease organisms and pests such as aphid eggs and weed seeds. In buying composts you should make sure that the name, manufacturer and the ingredients are clearly stated.

You can do without soil

Plants do not absorb nutrients directly from the soil; these are first of all dissolved through the action of water and the presence of humus substances, and then they can penetrate the roots as liquid nourishment. As far as plants are concerned therefore, the soil is only a storehouse for nutrient salts and water and the anchorage in which they fasten their roots.

Several methods of culture which are increasingly being used in recent times, as against the cultivation of pot plants in soil, are based on this discovery; they include hydroponics and cultivation in various soil-less composts, principally peat, but also gravel.

Hydroponics

Through this technique the plants grow wholly without soil in a solution of nutrients. As the roots need to be anchored, they are placed in a perforated container which is filled with an inert material (gravel, broken brick, basalt chips, vermiculite, plastic flakes or fibres) and which is hung in a large watertight container filled with the nutrient solution.

In the house special vases of glass or glazed pottery are used, such as you find in garden shops; in theory, however, any watertight container with the appropriate insert can be used. In this way you can use flower troughs and plant bowls.

You can obtain the nutrient tablets, which have to be dissolved according to the directions, from a garden shop. Fill the container with the solution until the roots are half covered. There should be $\frac{1}{2}$"–1" (1–2 cm) of space between the inner container and the surface of the water so that sufficient air reaches the roots. Every three to four weeks the used solution should be poured away and a fresh one substituted; in between times fresh water is added as needed. In winter or in a definite resting period the concentration of nutrients should be lowered and you should use about half the quantity.

Soft lime-free water is best for the preparation of the solution and for topping up, for lime combines with nutrient salts in a form which cannot be absorbed by the plant's roots. The plants sicken and show signs of deficiency. Also you must make sure that the nutrient solution and the water are always brought to room temperature; otherwise your plants will suffer a shock from the cold liquid.

Hydroponics makes life simpler

Hydroponics makes the care of house plants much simpler, chiefly because in this way you avoid making mistakes in fertilizing and watering, and you can leave the plants to themselves for a long time, in some circumstances for as long as three to four weeks, provided the water supply lasts. You can find this out by observation over a long period.

The usual requirements for healthy plant growth—light, warmth and moisture—must also be provided. Even temperatures are particularly important for plants grown in water containers, for in contrast to soil and other growing media the nutrient solution does not adjust to falls in temperature very well (see 'Plants suffer from "cold feet" too', page 12).

Difficulties of Adaptation

Not all plants react favourably to this method of culture—most green plants are particularly suited to it—they must

Philodendron and Swiss Cheese plant also do well if they are grown by the method known as hydroponics. The plants stand in a perforated inner container, and the ends of the roots dip into the nutrient solution in the outer container. This container can be of watertight glazed earthenware, of plastic or of coloured glass. Clear glass is not recommended as algae are more inclined to settle in it. The outer container should always be only half or at most two-thirds filled with the nutrient solution, so that the roots also have sufficient air to breathe.

21

Plants which are to be grown by hydroponics must be slowly accustomed to this method from extreme youth. There is no point in trying the experiment three days before you go on holiday! However, anyone who has kept house plants by this method for some time can cheerfully go away for several weeks—the plants will look after themselves during his or her absence.

Pumice chips and broken brick often contain a great deal of lime which is harmful to plants. If you decide to use them, you must remove this lime beforehand, using sulphuric acid (one part of sulphuric acid to ten parts of water). N.B.: Handling sulphuric acid is dangerous: you must use containers which are absolutely acid-proof and should pour the sulphuric acid, drop by drop, into the water and never the other way round, otherwise it will splutter and the splashes cause burns. Finally you must rinse very thoroughly with clean water.

Peat contains 90% organic constituents, principally sphagnum moss which decomposes very slowly. Potting media based on peat always remain loose, crumbly and aerated; and they hold water well.

also be acclimatized to it from the beginning, and so they should be introduced to it as seeds or cuttings. Older plants which are growing in soil find it hard to adjust. You can try it with healthy young plants by rinsing the roots gently in lukewarm water and then carefully introducing them, if possible without damage, into the plant container. After the transfer you should keep them in plain water for a few days before filling up with the solution.

Cultivation in various media
The rearing of plants in various inert substances such as shingle, sand, brick fragments, pumice chips, plastic flakes or fibres, is merely a variation of hydroponics. The only difference is that you set the plants in one of these media in a large watertight bowl; often too they are put into individual pots filled with the medium and placed in a large trough which is filled with water and nutrient solution according to need. For this method gadgets for adding and removing water are necessary and also a water-level indicator. You can make it all automatic—a wide field for the professional or the keen amateur inventor.

Peat is kind to plants
Cultivation in peat constitutes a true middle way between soil and water culture. Peat is a substance which plants like and which is obtained from the surface of high moorlands. It consists of dead but not decayed plant materials, chiefly of sphagnum moss; it is stacked in big heaps, dried, broken up into small pieces and then pressed into bales. Its most important quality from the plant's point of view is its structure: peat can take up to twenty times its own weight of water and store it without becoming waterlogged and thereby depriving the roots of the air they need. Peat contains hardly any nutrients, but it does have a high proportion of the humus-forming salts which are so necessary to plants. From this comes its ability to store inorganic nutrients and to offer them to the plant in a form it can accept, to 'puff them up' as the gardener says. Even the harmful lime content of hard tap water is neutralized by peat. For these reasons peat has been used in horticulture in many ways for a long time (standard composts and other potting soils also contain a high proportion of peat). It is available in the trade as pure peat in finer or coarser fibre structures and as various peat

mixtures which consist of peat with the addition of a precise quantity of inorganic nutrient salts according to the purpose for which it is to be used, e.g., Levington compost.

You can therefore grow your plants either in pure peat or in a peat mixture and, according to need, you water either with pure water or with a nutrient solution—this would be a variant of hydroponics. You can, however, also use these mixtures as an addition to potting soil in order to break it up and at the same time to improve its capacity to store water and absorb inorganic nutrient salts.

Peat and soil-less composts must be well dampened before they are used for plants. If you squeeze a handful, water should run out. Pure peat is often reluctant to absorb water—a few drops of a wetting agent (washing-up liquid) help and won't harm the plants.

Feeding is simple these days

Whether your plants are growing in potting compost or in peat with fertilizer, in either case they will need additional nutrients after a little while if they are to grow and bloom for longer than a few weeks. There are as many (or perhaps even more) special recipes for "correct" feeding as there are for soil-mixing old-style.

Luckily the housewife who has only a couple of pot plants and the flower trough on the balcony to look after need not worry about something which is of the utmost importance to nurseries, agricultural undertakings or even the dedicated amateur gardener who wishes to grow his own fruit and vegetables. However, there is no need for him to research into the science of the effect of individual nutrients on plants and their influence upon each other. There's no need for him either to make experiments with traditional home-made remedies, which are seldom of use and more often than not unattractive and worthless, if not downright harmful to plants—stinging nettle tea, for instance, fermented pigeon's dung, eggshell water, coffee grounds or even salad oil. Today's chemical industry offers for home use a large number of compound fertilizers containing the various nutrient salts which house plants need, in the correct proportions, including all the trace elements.

This kind of fertilizer, which can also be added as the stock feeding substance to peat mixtures and standard composts, comes in liquid form or as a powder which is easily dissolved in water. Sometimes food sticks or balls are available; these you simply stick into the damp soil. They are perfectly effective, but it is somewhat difficult to get the dosage right. Of course it costs more to buy these instant fertilizers than it does to mix them yourself from basic ingredients, but it is worth it for their convenience and accuracy; in any case the

It is not particularly essential to know this, but it is interesting: compound fertilizers are composed of N = nitrogen (brings about strong rapid growth, bright green leaf colouring; if too much is given, the plant grows too luxuriantly, the leaves are soft and limp, and flowers fail to form), K$_2$O potassium (it makes the cell structure stable, maintains the chlorophyll content, furthers the formation of flowers and helps the plant to resist frost), P$_2$O$_5$ = phosphorus (encourages root growth and flower formation). The amount of the individual chemicals is given on the packet of compound fertilizer using these letters as well as percentage figures. Special fertilizers for house plants contain minute quantities of boron, copper, iron, manganese, zinc, cobalt, molybdenum and other trace elements, the presence of which is of great importance to the plant's vital processes.

quantities you will need for domestic use are really not very large.

It does not matter whether you buy a liquid manure or a soluble powder. In either case you should make sure that you are getting a compound fertilizer with trace elements and that full details of the manufacturer and of the formula are given on the packet.

There are special preparations for individual, highly sensitive types of plant such as azaleas, cacti, bromeliads and orchids; compound fertilizers are, however, suitable for the majority of pot plants. Beginners will do best to keep to the products of well-known firms which cannot afford to endanger their reputations by marketing dubious, insufficiently tested products. You should try fertilizers of unknown origin on expensive plants only with the greatest caution, if at all.

What is the correct way to fertilize?

Caution is recommended here too. The principle of giving a little extra just for luck does not work in this case—quite the opposite: too much fertilizer can cause irremediable damage. On the other hand too little fertilizer may have a slight effect on the plant's growth, but this can very quickly be rectified by increasing the quantity of fertilizer given.

Basically you feed only healthy plants which show by the development of new leaves, shoots and buds that they are in their growing period. Dormant plants which are not growing and may even be losing their leaves should not be fed. Most of our indoor plants go through this rest period in the winter when the temperature is low and they receive less light, but there are house plants with a summer resting period; for instance, amaryllis and several leaf cacti.

Other plants yet again, foliage plants in particular, hardly have a resting period at all. They even grow in winter, if they stand in a warm and relatively light position or are given artificial light (see page 9). Contrary to the old rule, these plants should be fed in winter, but of course only with half rations.

In preparing the fertilizer solution you should always follow the instructions which are usually given with reputable products, or which can be obtained if need be from the firms concerned. You should always, particularly at the beginning, err on the side of under- rather than over-feeding.

Generally it is better and more beneficial to the plants to

feed them frequently but only with a weak solution. There is always the danger with too high a concentration of fertilizer that the roots will be scorched (the nutrient salts will draw the water out of the roots instead of penetrating the plants in a soluble form).

For this reason you should never water a plant with a fertilizer solution if the soil ball in the pot has dried out too much. Plants which have dried out must be placed in tepid water for half an hour (see page 17) and should not be fed until a few days later when they have recovered.

The plant's requirements in the way of food vary according to the type of plant, its size, state of development and the size of its pot; young plants which are still growing need more than old, fully developed specimens. Unfortunately there is no single miracle recipe which is suitable for them all. You must observe the plants attentively instead.

As the formulae of commercial compound fertilizers, though similar, are not identical, it is a good idea to change the brand occasionally in order to cancel out any deficiency in one area or another.

Chemical reaction of the soil

Whether or not the roots can take up the fertilizer and make good use of it depends to some extent on the composition of the soil and the lime content (the hardness) of the water. In this connection the pH value of the soil plays a role. The scientist uses pH to measure the chemical reaction of a solution of soil which may be more or less acid or alkaline. There is a scale of pH values extending from 1 to 14. The neutral point is pH 7, numbers above that indicating an increasing alkalinity, and those below a corresponding acidity. Lime changes the soil reaction to an alkaline one and moreover lime combines with certain important plant nutrients to form chemical compounds which cannot be taken in by the roots or which may even be positively harmful.

Most plants favour a medium to weak acid reaction in the soil, between 5 and 6·5 pH; some, such as rhododendrons, azaleas, heathers, camellias, like a strongly acid soil, round about 4 pH, while others, such as cacti, prefer a slightly alkaline reaction between 7 and 8 pH. Plant life is no longer possible above 9 pH.

Standard and soil-less composts are adjusted to the pH values which are acceptable to plants; pure peat is very acid in its reaction. It is therefore added to the growing media of acid-

Cyclamens, which usually get thrown away when they have finished blooming, can be made into almost continuously flowering plants which will keep going all year long in the house, if you feed them correctly. You buy them in full bloom from the nursery in autumn or winter. If they are kept in a not too warm place, fertilized fairly sparingly but regularly, they will not lose their leaves and will bloom again after a short rest period in the summer.

The shrimp plant grows and flowers nearly the whole year through, provided it stands in a light place and is regularly fertilized.

If you want to know the exact pH value of a soil, you can buy a soil testing kit at your seed merchant's. This is a liquid which is added, drop by drop, to a specimen of the soil dissolved in water: it changes colour according to the lime content. With the help of the accompanying colour scale, you can read off the values.

Two substances have proved themselves in making the earth in flower pots looser and therefore more aerated: peat (the coarser, more crumbly version if possible) and in recent years vermiculite, a naturally occurring substance which, when treated, produces air-filled granules.

If the soil in the flower pot becomes hard, if moss and algae settle on the surface, if a white bloom and dirty incrustations appear on clay pots, then people often say that the soil has gone sour. The fault is, however, too high a concentration of lime.

loving plants (see above) and it can combine with excess lime and so neutralize an alkaline reaction to a certain extent.

Can soil "go sour"?

Planted by gardeners or by us in standard potting composts or soil-less composts, plants find the pH value suited to them. If, however, they are watered for a considerable period with hard water, more and more lime becomes concentrated in the soil, and the pH value is pushed up into the unfavourable alkaline reaches of the scale. At the same time fertilizer residues which cannot be utilized by the plants also collect. These show themselves on the outside of clay pots as white, grey or yellow deposits, and at times you even find them on the surface of the potting medium. The plants no longer grow properly, the roots die off, and the leaves become discoloured and turn yellow and finally brown and brittle.

Inexperienced plant lovers, believing that the plants are suffering from lack of water, then water even more and make a bad situation even worse. In compost which is waterlogged all the time, the roots receive no further air and they begin to rot, and algae and moss invade. Then you hear people say, "The soil has turned sour," though in reality it is suffering from too much lime.

The only remedy for these plants, if it is not too late, is to take them out of their pots at once, to remove all the dead roots and the old exhausted soil as much as possible, and to plant them in a new pot which is not bigger, but smaller than before, in fresh compost or medium; and then to water them with extreme care, using only rain or soft water, and not to feed until the plants have visibly recovered.

In this area prevention is better than cure—it is for this reason that it is so important to inform yourself fully about the degree of hardness of your tap water, if you cannot obtain guaranteed soft rain water, and to treat the water accordingly (see page 18). In hydroponics, in particular, the soil cannot possibly go sour, but water with a high lime content can have very damaging effects.

Plant Containers

The familiar old, you might almost say classic, flower pot of reddish-brown unglazed clay was for a long time the solitary lord of the window sill. In recent times, however, plant containers are being offered increasingly in all kinds of other materials—plexiglas, plastic, expanded polystyrene and other man-made materials, porcelain, glazed pottery and metal. Do these make the clay pot unnecessary, or is old faithful still the best, or even, as many people claim, the only pot really fit for its job?

The faithful clay pot

The clay pot has certain incontestable advantages: it is available all the time in many standard sizes, it is easily stacked, its earthy colour goes well with all plants and, above all, it is cheap—it is not a disaster if every now and then a pot is broken.

Possibly one characteristic is a disadvantage, although the clay pot's supporters consider it essential for successful pot plant cultivation: the unglazed, once-fired clay is porous, it lets water and air pass from the interior to the exterior and vice versa. This is good, say the supporters, for only in this way do the roots in the flower pot receive sufficient air. The opposite view is this: in nature the air can penetrate the soil solely from above, and then only when the structure of the soil is loose and capable of holding air. If the pot is large enough and the potting compost is correspondingly loose, then the air which penetrates from above is sufficient for the roots in the flower pot.

When, on the other hand, the soil is spoiled through incorrect mixing or insufficient watering, then air which comes through the sides of the pot is no longer of use to the roots. The clay pot's characteristic of letting air pass through it is therefore not actually harmful, but it is not essential either.

The dangers of chilling through evaporation

Equally controversial is the clay pot's property of letting water pass through. In a free standing clay pot the greater part of the moisture in the soil is not used by the plants but evaporates through the walls of the pot. As a result conden-

Geraniums, agaves, cacti and oleanders give the lie to the belief that plants need clay pots which allow air and water to pass in order to do well; in the south they grow and flower happily in jam jars, soup tureens and other containers not originally intended for this purpose.

Some of the water you give your plants evaporates through the walls of the clay pot. This evaporation causes a lowering of the temperature and a constant chilling of the roots of the plant.

By inserting a thermometer into the soil you can find out whether the plants are suffering from chilly roots.

A pot holder (cachepot) is not an unnecessary luxury, for it collects moisture-laden air between the clay pot and the outer container. The holder must be big enough for the clay pot to fit inside comfortably. There should be a space of about ½–¾" (1–2 cm) all the way round between the two pots. Three small stones in the outer pot will ensure that surplus water can run out of the clay pot.

sation causes a drop in temperature (you can really feel this if you take hold of a clay pot) with this result—that the root section is chilled, which from the plant's point of view is dangerous. Measurements, which anyone can check with a simple thermometer, have shown that the temperature of the soil in a clay pot lies several degrees below the general room temperature. The variation becomes even greater if the air directly round the pot becomes warmer and dryer and a greater amount of water evaporates through the walls of the pot. The danger is therefore particularly great in winter.

One result of evaporation is that you must water more often and more generously, and, beside the extra work, this means that the soil will become impregnated with lime even more quickly and severely than usual, if you are using hard water. The potting compost will become exhausted more quickly because of these deposits and must be changed more frequently (see 'Chemical reaction of the soil', page 25). Finally, fertilizer salts and lime will dissolve in the water, and will then be carried through the walls of the pot and deposited on the outside. The pot will become covered with unsightly growths, spots and incrustations.

Useful pot holders

Centuries ago the unaesthetic appearance of the clay pot brought about the fashion of using pot holders (cachepots); these, properly managed, can overcome the other disadvantages of the clay pot. They must be properly used; the pot holder should be big enough for the pot to sit comfortably inside, and for you to be able to take it out with ease in order to check that no excess water has collected underneath to give the plants a harmful cold bath (see page 17). Between the clay pot and the pot holder there is a zone of moist air which prevents any further, potentially harmful evaporation. Now and then it is recommended that you fill the space between the pot and the pot holder with damp peat; this has hardly any significance from the point of view of evaporation and the moisture content of the air, but, on the other hand, it does prevent your keeping an accurate check on the amount of water given. It is quite another matter when you place several flower pots in a large container (a plant trough, for instance; see page 31) and pack the intervening spaces with peat or some other filling material. Then the porosity of the clay pot is an advantage, for the water only passes through in one direction as it is required. In this way you can give the plants an additional reserve of water by keeping the peat damp and you will not need to water so often. Changes of temperature and chilling of the roots will also be largely avoided.

Which shape is correct?

Two other features of the clay pot are often put forward indiscriminately as being necessary to plants: its conical shape, tapering in at the bottom, with its somewhat thick rim, and the drainage hole in its base. The shape is the result of the method of manufacture and of its use in the nursery garden where empty pots need to be stacked in as little space as possible and easily transported. It is not entirely favourable to the roots of plants; the natural root ball which plants form when they are not squeezed into pots is seldom long and tapering (only a few pot plants, such as some kinds of palm, have tap roots) but more often shallow and wide-spreading (these plants do best in bowls), and in most cases the root ball is round. Containers with straight vertical sides are good for these; those with curved sides are even better but present too many difficulties when it comes to repotting.

Should the flower pot have a drainage hole?

The drainage hole in the bottom of the pot is not an unnecessary relic of the past but a safety valve: if by accident too much water is given, the water drains away without hindrance and can cause no further trouble, provided, of course, that the hole has not been blocked by soil, stones or roots. You can place a piece of broken pot or crock over the hole.

The drainage hole, however, does mean that something waterproof must be placed underneath if the pots are to stand in the house or on a balcony. The simplest solution is a tray or saucer of watertight glazed pottery, asbestos cement or plastic. It should be large enough and have a high rim, so that it can really catch the water—if it is too restricted in size, it will overflow. It looks prettier if the plants are placed in pot holders of the same kind, or when you arrange several together in a plant trough (see page 31).

Using containers without drainage holes

You *can* do without a drainage hole and saucer altogether, and this is the most modern and attractive solution.

Plants with spreading roots, such as the azalea, grow best in bowls.

Plants with a round soil ball, such as climbing figleaf palm, are equally as happy in containers with vertical sides as in the usual pots.

Plants with tap roots, such as the coconut palm, need a tall pot.

29

You need to get hold of watertight containers of glazed pottery, plexiglas, polystyrene or other plastic materials. This does demand a certain amount of experimentation in watering, for you can no longer check whether there is superfluous water collecting in the bottom.

The pots should be rather large for this method and it is particularly useful if they are deep, as then you can build up a drainage layer in the bottom, about 1″ (2–3 cm) thick. You can use gravel for this, or, even better, vermiculite flakes, which are feather-light, practically rot-proof and hold the air. These flakes are now being mixed with some of the potting composts to make them looser and improve their air-holding qualities. You should always use them, if possible, in these watertight containers. You should also make sure that the potting medium has a coarse grained texture, with plenty of air, so that it will not turn into cement when it is wet (mix in fibrous peat).

Plastics, polystyrene and plexiglas have yet another advantage: they are bad conductors of heat, and there will be no condensation on the outside. Inside the container the roots always enjoy an even temperature. Porcelain and clay pots, on the other hand, conduct heat comparatively well; if they stand on a cold marble window sill or directly in a cold draught, your plants may "catch cold". One disadvantage of all watertight containers is that, apart from some not very attractive pots of polystyrene or simple plastic, they are rather expensive. As the plants grow, sooner or later you will have to buy either a new pot or a new plant, so it is worthwhile providing a big enough pot from the beginning.

This is the way to set about planting in a watertight container: you need, at the bottom, a drainage layer of gravel or vermiculite which should be at least an inch (2–3 cm) deep—2″ (5 cm) and more for large containers; above this you place coarse fibrous peat or peat compost, well dampened; and finally the plant with its soil ball.

Plant Troughs

You can make plant care in the house very much easier and also provide better living conditions for the plants if you don't install a large number of single pots but put the plants together in one spot in the room. This may be a window garden, but there are other ways of creating a garden within the house.

Many architects call a window garden something which, in most cases, is no more than an extra-wide window sill. If this window is in the living room, facing south, with no protection against the sun and perhaps with a radiator underneath, then looking after plants will be an exceedingly exhausting and unsuccessful business.

Plant troughs are easy to look after

Simplifying the work involved begins with a plant trough— i.e., a large, watertight container in which you can place several plants in their pots. Even a simple tray or a baking tin with a high rim can fulfil this function. If you fill it with gravel and in it place the plants (in pots with drainage holes), then you can water them all in one go. The constant evaporation of water from the bed of gravel (you can also use peat, but it doesn't look so attractive) creates a microclimate which is much appreciated by the plants: a cloak of damp, coolish air which enwraps the plants and lessens their demand for water.

Better than this simple solution, which is really little more than an extra-large saucer, is a plant trough with a depth of at least 3″ (6 cm), made of plastic, non-porous wood (with a lining), zinc or asbestos cement. Plant troughs are now available in many different shapes and sizes, with or without legs, in wood, plastic or asbestos cement, in department stores, furniture shops, seed merchants and garden centres. In some cases you can even have them made to measure— or, if you are a clever do-it-yourselfer, you can make them out of wood with a waterproof lining of thick plastic or plastic paint.

An even better method: hiding the pots completely

A system which is even more effective and kinder to the plants is for the plant trough to be so deep that the pots can

Even a shallow plant tray makes the work of caring for your plants easier. The pots (with drainage holes) should stand on a layer of gravel, about an inch (2 cm) deep, in which water is always present.

Even better is a plant trough which is deep enough for the flower pots to be completely concealed inside it.

31

This is how the pots should be arranged in a deep plant trough: the large ones should stand on a drainage layer of gravel or vermiculite, the small ones should be supported by empty pots turned upside down. The base of the stem must always be in the open. The spaces between the pots should be filled with coarse peat.

Pots which are sunk up to their rims can be watered in the ordinary way from above, and the filling material only kept moderately damp. You can, however, also water them from underneath and fertilize them at the same time, provided all the pots are approximately the same size and all the plants have more or less the same requirements.

be sunk in it up to their rims. You can cover the soil surfaces evenly with gravel, large stones or peat and so give the impression that the plants are growing directly in the soil. You fill the space between the individual pots with peat, soil-less compost, which will provide nourishment at the same time, or vermiculite. You can also use lime-free stones or coarse gravel, but with these even distribution of water is not guaranteed, and in addition the trough then becomes very heavy. Soil is not recommended either, for it also is too heavy and becomes waterlogged very quickly.

In plant troughs like these the clay pot proves its worth with its capacity for letting water pass through its sides. The pots must always have a drainage hole for only then will the benefit of watering all the plants at once be appreciated. No pot should stand directly on the floor of the plant trough (because of the danger of water collecting) and no plant should be set in so deeply that the base of the stem is covered by the filling material. You must therefore stand small pots on other upturned pots, if the compost does not provide sufficient support. If you fill the trough with peat or soil-less compost, it is a good idea to line the bottom with a drainage layer one to two inches (3–5 cm) thick. It may consist of coarse gravel or crocks; vermiculite is very suitable. When all the sunken pots are at about the same depth, you can water them in the trough from underneath and feed them in this way too. A water level indicator is useful—you can make one yourself from a piece of tube and a stick; so is a tap to run off excess water. Some ranges of ready-made troughs already have a water-level indicator built in and a tap for running off unwanted water.

Small pots which do not reach down to the water-carrying layer must be individually watered from above. This is a good plan too when your plant trough contains plants with varying water and fertilizer requirements. You can administer the water and nutrients individually. The filling material need be kept only moderately damp. Even at the beginning there is no need for it to be thoroughly wetted for any length of time.

Whether you water from above or from below, the plants in a trough always need less water than those in free-standing pots. It is often sufficient to water them once a week or even once a fortnight. You can also cope with quite long absences if you have a trough like this.

Planting without pots

Sometimes you will be advised to fill the trough with a soil mixture or a soil-less compost and place the plants straight into this without a pot. This is really only possible if you water with extreme care and do not omit the drainage layer. It is really only to be recommended when you change all the plants from time to time—for instance, in window-boxes and bowls of flowering plants which only last for one season.

There are difficulties, however, with an arrangement of plants which is to last throughout the year; the roots entwine and it becomes impossible to remove one plant, if it grows too big or if it is not developing properly, and to replace it with another. Changing the soil or potting medium which ought to be carried out at least once every one or two years, is then almost impossible, except with a great deal of work, dirt and damage to the plants.

Replacing the soil

At infrequent intervals, about once a year, the filling between the pots should be changed or cleaned, for dust, soil, dead plant material, deposits from watering and fertilizing, and often disease organisms, collect in it. Peat or soil-less compost is replaced by new. Gravel and vermiculite can be washed in clean water.

You can make a simple water-level gauge from a piece of hose or a tube and a stick which is placed inside. The principle is the same as for the oil dipstick in a car.

Window Gardens

A plant trough is the first step towards a window garden. The trough should be deep enough for the flower pots to be sunk inside it. If there is a radiator underneath, you should make sure that the warm air can reach the window pane as well as the interior of the room. The air should be moistened beforehand if possible. Shade from the sun is certainly an essential. It should be arranged outside the window as it is less effective on the inside.

A roomy plant trough is the first and most important requisite for a properly functioning window garden. As for the means employed and the plants which will be kept in it, much depends on whether you wish to install a glass screen between the window and the room, and special heating and watering equipment, possibly even an automatic system.

Built-in plant troughs

If you plan your window garden when the house is being built, then you can have the plant trough inserted into the brickwork. In this case you must make sure not only that the trough is absolutely watertight, but also that it is well insulated against the cold which will penetrate from outside through the masonry. Cracks in the brickwork and drainage holes which lead outside are sources of cold which will damage the roots of plants. If you do have a built-in trough which has not been properly constructed, your best plan is to prepare a somewhat smaller, waterproof insert of zinc or asbestos cement and to line the intervening space with insulating material. You can even install floor heating: this consists of insulated heating cables or of a wire mesh provided with a low voltage current through a small transformer. You can buy heating equipment of this kind in specialist garden shops.

It is particularly important that the heat should rise up the outside wall, and it is good too if a warm air current flows directly on to the window pane (provided, of course, that this air has been thoroughly moistened previously). In a new house you can direct the warm air from a radiator through slits so that the plant trough and the window garden are warmed (for means of moistening the air, see page 13).

A shade is nearly always essential

Window gardens which face south-east, south and west and which receive several hours of sunshine each day need proper protection from the sun through fabric or Venetian blinds which are fitted outside the window or, in double-glazed windows, between the two panes of glass.

A blind on the inner side of the window pane is always a makeshift arrangement which causes a great deal of work and annoyance, for the plants grow towards the light and rest against the pane, so that you can no longer make proper use of the blind.

If you do not value the view, you can have opal glass fitted. You must remember that this will lower the general intensity of the light, so you may need to install artificial light (see page 9).

Recently window glass has become available which has a layer on one side which is transparent and lets the sunlight through, but which also reflects back the heat rays so that they cannot penetrate the room. Whether this new material will make a blind for the window garden redundant remains to be seen.

Cleaning windows—a problem

When the plant window has been built in, there is always the problem of cleaning the windows. Even when you live in relatively dust-free surroundings and are really above such things, you cannot wholly ignore this job. If you cannot reach to clean the windows comfortably from outside, you should decide against a permanently fixed window garden and choose instead a movable plant trough which can be pushed out of the way for cleaning. The window is then no longer permanently closed but a normal room window which can be opened.

Anyone who wants to cultivate delicate tropical plants will need a glass screen to separate the plants from the room and heat, for these plants need moderately high temperatures and an air moisture content of at least 75%. A hygrometer, and soil and air thermometers will make it easier for you to keep a check on these.

Another solution for delicate plants or for those which have to stand in draughty halls and passages is a glass case or cloche which is placed over a plant trough. If these cases are placed at some distance from a window, they will need artificial lighting.

If you are planning a window garden, you must think about cleaning the window. The outside presents problems unless the windows are at ground level or open on to a balcony. The inside is always difficult with fixed panes, if you cannot shift the plants. You can help yourself by having casement windows which open outwards or by choosing to have several small troughs (instead of a big one) which you can easily move out of the way.

Repotting

According to their age, growth and condition plants will need fresh soil and a larger pot from time to time. Young, vigorously growing plants must be repotted every year, and many twice a year. Older or slow-growing plants, such as cacti, and other succulents, need a new pot only at an interval of some years. And of course when the soil or potting medium has been spoiled by the wrong kind of care, it is necessary to repot the plants.

Choosing the right moment

In an emergency you can repot at any time during the year. In general you repot healthy, vigorous plants at the beginning of the growing period, that is in early spring; with flowering pot plants some can be repotted after blooming in summer (for instance, camellias and azaleas). During the winter resting period you should not disturb the plants by repotting.

Check whether repotting is necessary

The best way to find out if a plant needs repotting is to take it briefly out of its pot. To do this you place the right hand over the pot so that the stem of the plant passes between your fingers, turn the pot upside down and tap it sharply on a table edge. In most cases you can then easily lift the pot off and have a look.

In many instances the roots are pressing so hard against the sides of the pot (only with clay pots) that the soil ball will not come out. Then you must ease it out with a knife blade, but, as in these cases a new pot is necessary, you may prefer to break the old one with a hammer and release the roots in this way.

Removing dead roots

If only small white root tips are visible, then the pot is still big enough, and you can simply replace the plant. If, however, you see a thick mesh of roots, a new and larger pot is needed. If there is a thick blanket of brown-coloured dead roots, you should loosen it with a sharpened stick or some other pointed implement and remove the dead roots. Of course, you should preserve healthy white roots as far as

This is the way you should hold the plant when you take it out of the pot: place your hand round the base of the stem, turn the pot upside down and tap it gently on the edge of a table. Then you can raise the pot from the soil ball and examine the plant to see whether it needs repotting.

When they have been repotted, the plants should not stand any deeper in the earth than they did before, or the base of the stem will rot. On the other hand, there should be a distance of half an inch (1½–2 cm) between the soil level and the rim of the pot to allow for watering. If the soil ball rises above the edge of the pot, then the water will run uselessly away.

36

possible. Plants whose soil balls have grown smaller are given fresh soil only, but not a bigger pot. If at the same time you somewhat reduce the upper part of the plants, by removing individual twigs and leaves (this is not possible with all plants), then they will survive this operation better.

How big should the new pot be?

Healthy plants are not cut back. They are given a new pot, which has a diameter about an inch (2–3 cm) larger than the old. The ball is only loosened if the roots are very thick or if the soil is very tightly packed round it; in most cases you can leave it undisturbed. You place some new earth in the pot, position the soil ball on it and fill the gap at the sides evenly with earth. Soil-less composts are made firm with a finger or a stick; with standard potting composts, it is sufficient to give the pot a sharp tap.

After repotting

After being repotted the plants should be given a single, generous dose of water at room temperature so that the soil or compost settles firmly round the roots. (Don't forget to dampen peat or soil-less composts well before use!) After this you should water with extreme caution for about two weeks, giving only enough to keep the soil from drying out. Plants which are intended to take their water from underneath should still be watered from above from time to time during the first four to six weeks, until they are fully accustomed to absorbing water from underneath.

As for fertilizing, you should wait until the plants show by their vigorous growth that they have recovered from the upheaval. Standard and soil-less composts already contain a supply of nutrients which will last for several weeks.

If only a few white root tips are visible, there is no need yet to repot (see above). If a great many roots can be seen, however, then the plant needs a new pot (see below). Any thick mesh of brown, dead roots must be loosened and removed as far as possible before you place the plant in fresh soil.

Propagation

The spider plant (Chlorophytum) forms young plants on the end of long runners. Simply put these in small pots to obtain new plants.

New plants come into being partly by seminal propagation (that is, through seeds) and partly by vegetative propagation (through cuttings, shoots or offsets and division). Both methods of increasing your stock can be undertaken in the house. They do not necessarily succeed with all plants, and conditions must be favourable, but the attempt will give you pleasure, and plants you have raised yourself often do better later on, as they have been accustomed to the climate of your room from the beginning.

Shoots

The easiest method for the indoor gardener is the propagation of plants which form shoots, such as Bryophyllum, spider plant, saxifrage, bromeliads and agave. In such species, young plants develop in the leaf axils, at the side of the stem or on long runners; these new plants already have roots, even though they are still attached to the mother plant. You only need to take the young plants and plant them in appropriately small pots, using standard or soil-less compost (mixed with sharp sand in the case of succulents).

Division

Equally simple is the division of many plants which have no main stem but which grow in a shrub-like form, like mother-in-law's tongue or umbrella plant. You take these plants out of the soil, and using a sharp knife, cut away part of the stems and put them in new pots.

Cuttings

Propagation by cuttings is somewhat more difficult. Many plants need special treatment, which the gardener can provide in a greenhouse, before they develop proper roots. However, it can succeed in the home with many foliage plants and cacti and with some flowering plants (see the survey of plants).

You can use shoots or part of the stem for this (rubber plants, tradescantia, fuchsia, geranium, cacti) or leaves (African violet and some types of begonia). Stem cuttings from foliage plants are cut off just below a leaf joint (about four to six leaves should remain on the cutting). With cacti you

This is how you make stemcuttings from tradescantia: cut off the tips of shoots with five or six leaves just below a leaf joint and stick into damp soil-less compost.

can use individual spikes which are easily separated (these are stems which have taken on a leaflike appearance, the actual leaves in cacti having been transformed into spines). Leaf cuttings are raised from individual, well-developed leaves; you nick or score the main rib several times and then lay the leaf flat on the soil.

Most cuttings root quickest in dampened soil-less compost; with plants that rot easily (like cacti or African violets) it is better to use a mixture of soil-less compost and sand.

With some plants which have woody stems, such as the rubber plant and swiss cheese plant, you can use the air-layering technique. You cut half way through the stem just below a leaf, jam a tiny stone between the cut edges so that they do not grow together again, and pack a handful of well-dampened sphagnum moss or coarse peat round the cut surfaces. A plastic bag goes over the top and is tied firmly with bass above and below the cut. After four to six weeks you will see whether roots have formed (in between times you must check whether the moss or peat is still moist). If they have, cut off the top of the plant and plant it with its roots in potting compost. One desirable side effect is that the original plant forms one or more new shoots out of the "eyes" below the cut.

All cuttings grow better if they are covered with a glass or a plastic bag.

Warmth and high humidity favour root growth in all cuttings. You should therefore place the little pots in a warm spot, but not directly in the sunlight, and slip a plastic bag, supported on sticks, or a glass over them. Beneath this hood there is a build-up of air which is saturated with moisture and which prevents the plants from losing water through evaporation and from drying out, and protects them until they can provide themselves with water through their new roots.

On the other hand, in order to prevent rotting and diseases, you must lift this hood each day for a short while. When you observe that the plants have formed roots—they begin to grow and to put out new leaves—you can accustom them to the air of your room by removing the hood each day for increasingly longer periods.

Growing plants from seed

Propagating plants from seed in the home is very difficult with many plants, for you cannot provide the intensity of light and the often very high temperatures required which the gardener can in his hot-house. All the same, you can

Leaf cuttings from an African violet: a new plant results from a well-formed leaf which has been cut off and placed in a mixture of sand and peat.

39

This is how you prick out: with a pointed stick you dig out the tiny plant with its minute soil ball and place it by itself in a small pot with John Innes Potting Compost No. 1 or a soil-less compost. You dig a small hole with the stick beforehand and carefully make the earth firm round the little plant with the stick.

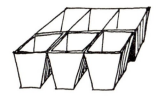

These small pots for growing plants have been pressed out of peat. You do not need to repot the young plants, but simply place them according to their stage of growth in larger pots, for the peat pots can be pierced by the roots and will gradually break down.

raise some flowering plants for your balcony or window-box very successfully indoors; cacti and coleus can be grown from seed indoors, as well as many kitchen herbs.

The seed packet which you buy at the seed merchant's usually gives adequate information about times of sowing and also tells you whether the plants should first be grown indoors before being planted out or whether they can be sown directly into the soil in which they are to grow.

For germination the seeds should be sprinkled as thinly as possible on well-dampened, soil-less seed compost in boxes or pans and should then be placed in a very light, but not sunny, place. Humid air favours the process of germination, but as soon as the little plants begin to come through, you must give them plenty of fresh air.

When the third or fourth leaf appears, the plants should be separated, either by thinning out the unwanted ones or through pricking out.

Even those plants which have been sown in the place where they are to grow should be thinned out slightly if they come through very thickly; they will then develop better.

Special pots for propagation

Little plastic pots which are fastened together to a tray with a common base into which water can be poured, or other pots pressed out of peat by a special process, all available in various sizes, are especially suitable for propagation.

All young plants, whether they have been raised from seed or cuttings, must be watered with great care and observation during their early days. Too much moisture is as harmful as the occasional drying out. Feeding is not necessary during the first weeks.

Pests and Diseases

Plant diseases, whether they are caused by fungi, bacteria and viruses or by insect infestation, are always a warning signal: something is wrong with the treatment the plant is receiving. Of course pests and diseases are always present, but healthy, well-cared-for plants, which are growing in the right place, survive their attacks without visible signs of severe damage and without our help.

The underlying cause is usually incorrect treatment

When a plant suddenly becomes sick, you should not only combat the visible symptoms with chemical and mechanical means, but should also investigate the underlying causes. Is the plant standing in the wrong place? Is it subject to falls in temperature or to draughts? Has it been kept too dry or too damp? Is the soil exhausted? Is its position too hot or too cold? All these factors upset plants' powers of resistance, and only when they have been worked out correctly, will the plants regain their health.

Don't hang on to them at all costs

It is worthwhile considering whether there is any point in continuing to care for a severely diseased plant. If the main part of the plant is badly affected, then it is better to get rid of it—a window-sill full of crippled plants gives no one any pleasure! Often, however, the plant may have some sentimental value, and then you will want to try to save it; the best way is by regeneration—by taking cuttings from the healthy twigs.

Look out for the first signs!

The most important measures in fighting plant diseases are, of course, adequate feeding and intelligent care. Prevention is always better than cure, and proper observation at the right time can prevent a great deal of harm. If the leaves change their usual position or their colour, suddenly droop limply, crinkle or curl up, or develop yellowish, white or brownish spots, these can all be signs of disease. A thorough inspection of the plant, perhaps with the help of a magnifying glass, is necessary in order to diagnose the malady in its beginnings.

Pests and diseases nearly always attack only the plants which have been weakened by incorrect treatment, too little light or wrong temperatures.

Weeping fig

Strong healthy plants in the right position hardly ever fall sick.

*Plant remedies which carry this symbol
have been officially approved by the
Agricultural Chemicals Approval Scheme
for safety and efficiency.*

*Insecticides are divided into two
groups: contact and systemic. The first
act as a contact poison—i.e., all insects
die when they come into contact with
the poison. The others are taken up
by the roots or leaves of the plant and
are carried by the sap into all the stems
and leaves. They act on insects which
suck the sap or eat parts of the leaves,
even when they are protected from direct
contact with the insecticide by a thick
shield (scale insects) or through tightly
furled leaves (some kinds of aphid).*

Plants are threatened both by insect infestation and by
actual diseases caused by microscopically small fungi, bacteria and viruses.

Commercial products

Fighting these pests and diseases has today, like feeding and
the provision of the proper potting medium, become a
simple matter. We no longer need, as in grandma's day, to
collect cigar butts to obtain nicotine, to work up a soft soap
lather and to take other rather unpleasant measures.

In every garden shop you will find a big choice of remedies
which have been tested and approved by the Ministry of
Agriculture, Fisheries and Food under the Agricultural
Chemicals Approval Scheme.

They are effective against insects (insecticides), against mites
(acaricides), against slugs and snails (molluscicides) and
against fungus diseases (fungicides). There are also compound preparations which combat insects and fungus diseases at the same time, and others you can mix together
according to your needs.

Not every preparation is suitable for all plants, and the
effect is not always the same in every case. Before your experiment fruitlessly, you should let the professional advise
you, after you have fully described the plants and the symptoms which are to be treated. In general you will obtain this
advice from the nurseryman or seed merchant; in particularly difficult cases you can make inquiries of a horticultural
institute or advisory officer. (Incidentally, you may not
know that each county has a horticultural advisory officer,
usually attached to the county Department of Education.)
The most convenient products to use in the house are those
which are sold in aerosol containers. A single press on the
button will suffice to surround the whole plant with a fine
protective mist. This convenience is, however, purchased
at a relatively expensive price. It is cheaper, though a little
more fiddly to prepare, to buy water-soluble products
which can be used in a hand spray. Finally there are preparations in powder form which can be sprayed on straight
from the packet or from a little diffuser.

Be careful how you handle these preparations

Handling horticultural chemicals is not without danger.
Many contain fairly powerful poisons, while others are at
very least intolerable to both humans and animals. You must

therefore always take great care of these products so that there is no way for children to get hold of them. After use you must thoroughly cleanse yourself and the apparatus you have been using. Where possible, you should not dust or spray in the living-room (and certainly not in the kitchen), but in an infrequently used room or, even better, in the open air. In doing this you must watch out that no spray reaches your eye or is inhaled.

If you have a large number of plants to look after, the purchase of a small hand syringe is well worth while. With it you can spray the plants with chemicals very finely indeed.

Always follow the instructions!

Every plant chemical should carry complete instructions for use—that is the law. It is important to read them through properly and to follow them exactly, for only then can the treatment be successful. All parts of the plant must be carefully sprayed, with special attention to the under-sides of leaves and the places between the twigs which are hard to reach. The soil and the pot should be sprayed too. Places which are not treated are sources of further infection. It is nearly always necessary to repeat the treatment after eight to ten days, and often even a third time, for insect eggs, larvae and fungus spores often resist the spray and after a short while cause a fresh outbreak of the disease.

Overdoses and too high a concentration of plant protection chemicals can cause severe damage. If you are using aerosol cans, hold them at the right distance when you spray. The propellant gas, as it leaves the canister, evaporates causing a fall in temperature and considerable frost damage to the plants.

The principal animal pests

Thrips, an insect which is about a tenth of an inch (2–3 mm) in size, ranging from light to black in colour, with stumpy wings; it sucks at young leaves, buds and flowers. Grey-white specks on the leaves are the result and a characteristic silvery shine.

Greenfly—green, yellowish, brownish or black, a twelfth of an inch (1–2 mm) in size, often winged. They cluster, often thickly, on the under-sides of young leaves and on the still tender tips of shoots and flower buds, feeding on the plant's sap and giving off a sticky substance which is called "honey dew". Ants love honey dew and for this reason keep greenfly as "milch cows". The sticky spots on the upper sides of leaves are usually the first signs of greenfly attack. Often sooty moulds settle there too and turn the spots black. Greenfly can also carry virus diseases.

Scale insects—brownish, hemispherical shapes which cling tightly to stems and stalks, often to the thick veins of large

Scale insects principally attack hard-leaved plants. Tub plants which have winter quarters which are too warm and too dark often suffer them.

Clivia is one of the most rewarding and least delicate of house plants. It is hardly ever attacked by pests or diseases.

Poisoned bait helps against slugs. It is in the form of granules which are eagerly eaten by the slugs and which kill them.

Spider mites are not insects and are therefore not affected by many insecticides. Study the instructions or obtain a special product against mites (acaricide).

leaves and to the roots. Beneath these "shells" are concealed fully grown, immobile insects, while the tiny six-footed larvae are mobile. Scale insects and their larvae also suck plant sap and give off honey dew. They are hard to combat with chemical means alone because of their shells. The best plan is to pick them off carefully with a pointed object and then to spray them with an insecticide.

Slugs and snails—usually slugs which come at night. By day they hide in a cool, damp place in the potting soil, beneath the flower pot, in the filling medium of the plant trough. They betray their presence through the irregular holes they eat in young leaves, flowers and buds, and often too by their silvery trails of slime. You can collect the bigger ones at night, but a more certain method is to use the special slug baits.

Red spider mites—tiny little mites which can only be seen by very sharp eyes or with the help of a magnifying glass. The first sign of their presence is fine webs on the under-sides of leaves. The leaves attacked develop first yellowish and then dry spots and later fall off.

White fly—about 1/12" (1–2 mm) long, white, triangular, winged insects which are found on the under-sides of leaves and which fly off when the leaves are moved. The wingless larvae shelter beneath tiny shells and can resist most plant chemicals. For this reason a repeated attack at intervals of eight to ten days is needed.

Mealy bugs—1/16" (2–4 mm) long, these big mobile insects are covered with a fine white cottony covering of waxy threads. They are usually found in the leaf axils and beneath young leaves. They, too, feed on the sap of the plant and exude honey dew.

The principal fungus diseases

Genuine mildew—first, round whitish spots appear on leaves, stalks, buds and flowers and later a floury grey deposit covers the whole of the plant and gradually turns dark-grey or brown.

False mildew—similar appearance, but mostly occurring on

the under-sides of leaves. The threads of fungus penetrate the leaves and gradually destroy them.

Botrytis (mould)—a grey furry covering develops from irregular brown or black areas of rot on leaves and stems. Mould first affects only the dead parts of a plant (which, in order to lessen the danger of infection, you should be careful to remove!) but soon it will attack the living parts too if the air is too moist, or if sufficient light and warmth are not available and the plants are too close together.

Rust—this shows itself usually as circular rust-coloured spots on the under-sides of leaves which feel rough and scabby and after some time give off a powder. The leaves finally dry out and fall off.

Incurable diseases
There is no chemical help available, at least for the amateur, to deal with bacterial and virus diseases. In a minor attack the plants cure themselves, provided you carefully cut away the infected parts. Severely diseased plants must be thrown away. You should also, if possible, remove the soil or potting medium; pots and gravel must be disinfected before they are re-used: use a solution of permanganate of potash (pot. permang.) or ask your local gardening shop for advice.

All types of aphid and the red spider appear on house plants chiefly when the plants are standing in air that is too warm and dry. Draughts too can lead to aphid infestation.

Norfolk Island pine easily falls victim to mealy bugs if it is kept in too dark and warm a place.

Fungal diseases are usually the result of plants' standing in a position that is too cool, damp and dark.

You can "pickle" seeds and flower bulbs against bacterial and viral diseases. Suitable products are available in liquid or powder form in seed merchants' shops —follow the instructions exactly!

When You Go Away

How do house plants fare when their owner has to go away for some time, and there is no friendly neighbour who can be asked to water the flowers?

Hydroponics makes you independent

Plants which have been kept by the method described on page 20 (hydroponics) survive quite happily for two to four weeks without being watered or receiving any attention. Of course, you must have observed them very carefully for a long time beforehand to establish how often additional water is needed and should suspend them, circumstances permitting, in a larger container for the period of your absence. You can also lower the plant's water requirements to some extent by keeping it as cool as possible and not placing it in a light room—even a plant grown by hydroponics will not survive a long holiday absence on a sunny window-sill.

In a plant trough like this the plants have a reserve of water for several weeks.

Plant troughs store water

The same thing applies to plants which are set in a plant trough. If, the evening before you go away, you water them plentifully for once from above and also dampen the filling medium thoroughly (for this purpose you can safely exceed the usual quantity, for in nature too plants receive an excess of water occasionally), then for two to three weeks in general they will keep going without being watered, depending on the size of the trough and on the humidity and temperature of the place where they are. In this case too it is a good idea to run an experiment or two beforehand and to provide a cool dark room for the plants during your absence.

Clay pots need extra help

Plants which are growing in individual clay pots are endangered by a long weekend, unless they are accustomed to drought conditions like cacti, succulents and the indefatigable sansevieria.

For a matter of several days a pot holder, half-filled with water, helps. If, however, your absence is to be longer than this, you must construct a temporary plant trough for these

There is a cheap temporary method which helps for about a week or even longer in cool weather: you water the pot plant well first (soaking it is even better) and then envelop it in a watertight plastic bag, pour some more water on to the earth and then tie the bag loosely round the plant with a piece of bast.

46

plants and this too should be placed in a cool, shady room, preferably one facing north (it should not be too dark and it certainly should not be the cellar!).

Water the pots freely for once or stand them in water for half an hour until no more air bubbles rise; then sink them right up to the rims of the pots in well-dampened peat. The earth in the pot should also be covered with a thick layer of peat, about 1″ (1–2 cm) in depth.

The water reserves will be even bigger if you stand the pots on small stones so that an inch or so of water (several centimetres) can stand in the bottom of the trough. The peat gradually absorbs this water from underneath and passes it on to the plants through the sides of the pots.

Any large watertight container can serve as a plant trough; if you have a well-lit bathroom, then use the bath. However, you should line it with a sheet of waterproof plastic before you put the peat in. Otherwise the enamel may suffer permanent marks and discoloration.

Using yarn as a wick

Another possibility for a long period of automatic watering is the wick method. For this you introduce one or more lengths of thick wick-like wool or cotton yarn, according to the size of the plant, into the soil in the pot. The other end of the yarn hangs down into a bucket of water. The yarn soaks the water up and carries it, as it is needed, to the soil. You can give each plant its own water supply or can link several to a bucket or a large bowl.

You should set up this wick-watering system some days before you go away so that you can make sure that the water supply is functioning properly—not all yarn carries water equally well, and the water may drip from the yarn where it sags.

You can place the pots next to the container and run the yarn into the pots from above, or you can place them on a wire rack over the water source and pass the wick from underneath up through the drainage holes (fasten it firmly, preferably with a splinter of wood so that it does not slide out). In the latter instance the plants also benefit from the moist air which rises from the surface of the water.

Other methods of automatic watering

There is a small gadget which you can buy at seed shops which works on a similar principle. It consists of a porous

Pieces of absorbent yarn act as water conductors. Make sure that the yarn reaches to the bottom of the supply container, as the water level will gradually go down. The best thing is to weight the yarn down with small stones.

47

With several special gadgets of the porous-cone type you can keep a whole plant box supplied with water for a long period.

cone of earthenware which is soaked in water and is then pressed into the soil in the pot. The cone is closed at the top with a plastic bung from which a transparent tube hangs, leading to a big container of water. When the earth in the pot dries out, the earthenware cone automatically soaks up fresh water.

You should also set up this apparatus a few days before your holiday, to see whether you have done everything properly and whether the water supply is working.

It is important that the end of the tube lies on the floor of the water container. You can use this method for all plants which cannot be moved. Even balcony flower-boxes can be watered in this way if you insert several cones at short intervals—but try it out first!

For individual plants the following method is thoroughly practicable. A glass or plastic bottle filled with water and fitted with a fine nozzle is turned upside down and pushed into the soil. It releases the water drop by drop according to the needs of the plant. You can find suitable bungs for all sizes of bottles.

Choice of Plants for the House

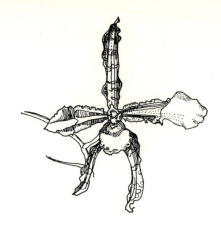

If you want to keep plants in the house successfully—and the previous chapters have demonstrated this—you must know and meet their individual requirements. It is then possible at all times to fulfil their needs as to soil, water, fertilizer and protection. It is up to the person looking after them to use his powers of observation to find out and do the right thing. It is difficult to match the factors of light, humidity and temperature to the actual needs of the plant. You cannot always provide artificial light or a sun blind just where you would wish (quite apart from the cost); you cannot turn the heating down so that the family freezes just for the sake of plants which need cool winter temperatures; similarly you could turn your home into a hot-house, with a humidity of 74%, for the benefit of some delicate tropical plants, but this would be very uncomfortable for people and unsuitable for furniture, books, clothing and foodstuffs.

In other words, if you don't want plants to order your entire life, then you must select them wisely and first of all check the conditions which a particular spot offers before you look for the plants which correspond with those living conditions.

One of the few orchids which, with careful treatment, will do well on a window sill is called Odontoglossum grande.

The circumstances existing in your house during the winter months will be the deciding factor in your choice. For this purpose the following lists of plants have been drawn up. Naturally they are not comprehensive; anyone with a little experience and an interest in experimenting can expand them considerably. But they can help to prevent beginners from suffering disappointments, and they can give a little encouragement to those who believe that, as far as house plants are concerned, they do not possess green fingers. In addition, professional gardeners are constantly engaged in taking new, hitherto unknown plants into their stock and in modifying old favourites by propagation to make them more suitable for the conditions obtaining indoors.

Finally there is a whole range of beautiful plants, mainly flowering plants, which to some extent you can continue to cultivate under particularly favourable conditions in your

Silky oak

Bougainvillea

living room, but which can also be considered as a kind of "bouquet in a pot": you buy them or receive them as a present in order to enjoy them for several weeks, and then you part with them when they have lost their beauty.

Bright and cool: the greatest choice

Araucaria excelsa (Norfolk Island pine)—this little fir tree with its regular growth needs temperatures of 50°F (10°C) and plenty of light in winter, and semi-shade and fresh air in summer (even in the open it needs protection).

Beloperone guttata (Shrimp plant)—this plant with its light green, heart-shaped leaves produces its white-green reddish brown bracts which so resemble hops nearly the whole year through, if it is allowed to stand in a light, but not too warm spot. Keep it well watered and feed generously.

Bougainvillea glabra and *spectabilis*—a familiar climber from Mediterranean countries with violet, red or pink flowers. In order to bloom the next season, it must pass through a rest period in winter at a temperature below 55°F (12°C); in summer it can stand in the sun on the balcony. In a warm room as a gift plant, discard after flowering.

Bryophyllum crenatum, *daigremontianum* and *tubiflorum*—unusual foliage plants with thick fleshy or rod-shaped leaves, on the edge or at the tip of which young plants are formed; these fall off easily and then grow separately. If Bryophyllum is kept in a bright cool place in winter, it will bear orange-red flowers. Keep it dry, and bring on new plants all the time, throwing away the old.

Rooms heated by a stove or open fire still provide light, cool conditions, though in modern dwellings with central heating such places have become rare: bright to sunny and with temperatures which in winter at least do not exceed 46–54°F (8–12°C) at night. If possible, by day too the room should be no warmer (shield from the fierce midday sun!) and only in exceptional circumstances should the thermometer rise over 59°F (15°C). Many plants prefer even lower temperatures still. They certainly do not die in higher ones, but they do not flower. It is important that the night temperature at least should be lower, so, if it is at all possible, you should switch the radiators off at night.

Cactaceae (Cacti—many kinds)—glove or drum-shaped, spiny or hairy or covered with a layer of wax—they love dry air, special composts with plenty of sand, very light positions, very little water. They can also stand high temperatures in winter but, in that case, do not bloom.

Camellia japonica—these beautiful shrubs with their double flowers of pinkish-red or white seldom come to anything because they cannot stand the climate caused by the central heating in modern houses. In winter they certainly need a

Bryophyllum

very bright, but not sunny, cool place, and moist air during the blooming period and the subsequent growing period. They must be kept evenly damp, but not wet (soft water is needed), and their pots must not be turned round, or the buds will drop. The best place for them in summer is a semi-shaded spot in the open.

Crassula portulacea—this forms bushes or miniature trees with a thick stem and round fleshy leaves. If it is kept in a very cool, bright condition in winter, it will form white star-shaped flowers. It can stand dryness and sunshine, but no heat in winter. It likes to spend the summer in the open air.

Cyclamen persicum—the old familiar and still one of the most popular flowering plants for the house. The handsome leaves with their silver-grey markings have decorative value too. If the cyclamen is kept in a cool, well lit spot and is regularly given a weak feed, it will keep going all the year through and will bloom almost without a break. Remove dead blooms and yellow leaves with a slight twist and a short tug, and do not pour water on to the crown! In a heated room you must consider them as one-season plants only and throw them away when they have finished blooming.

Cytisus canariensis and *racemosus*—these are kinds of broom with light green leaves and in spring are studded with yellow flowers. Cytisus only blooms again if it is kept very cool in winter (about 46°F, 8°C) in a well lit spot. Otherwise it must be considered a one-season plant and thrown away after blooming.

Echeveria (many kinds)—thickly leaved rosettes, frosted with blue-grey, green or hairy, producing shoots with orange or yellow star-shaped flowers. Water sparingly and keep cool in winter.

Euphorbia milii (Crown of Thorns)—a curiously growing plant with spiny twigs, small light green leaves and brilliant red blossoms from February to June. It can stand sunshine and dry air. It should be kept very cool in winter (it won't bloom in high temperatures). Water very cautiously and keep rather dry.

Blood flower

Passion flower

51

Rochea

Mother of thousands

Winter cherry

Grevillea robusta (Silky oak)—a foliage plant which grows like a shrub. It has light green graceful feathery leaves. It does not mind a relatively high humidity and somewhat warm position, up to 65°F (18°C). Water regularly and carefully.

Haemanthus albiflos, katharinae and *puniceus* (Blood flowers)—plants which are grown from bulbs and which have broad leaves and big white or red flowers. They can stand dry air and need a resting period from August to January during which they need only a little water.

Myrtus (Myrtle)—these graceful pot plants need a very bright, very cool position in winter and plenty of fresh air (air them on frostless days) and they should be given soft water. They enjoy spending the summer out of doors or at least by an open window.

Passiflora coerula (Passion flower)—this climber, with its interesting flowers which appear the whole summer through, needs plenty of light and sunshine, but it should be shielded in the house from the full glare of the midday sun. The lower the temperature in winter, the better the plant will bloom next summer.

Rochea coccinea—a succulent with fire-red umbels of flowers in summer. Bright to sunny position, cool in winter, but can spend the summer in the open. Likes dry air. Water sparingly in winter.

Saxifraga stolonifera (Mother of thousands)—with round leaves, silver grey veins, the under-sides tinged with red, and countless new plants on threadlike runners. Keep in a well-lit but not sunny place and water very carefully in winter.

Solanum capsicastrum (Winter cherry)—this is a kind of paprika, bush-shaped, with tiny dark green leaves and round or pointed red fruits in the autumn. The Winter cherry must be placed in a very light and airy position in summer, preferably in the open. In the house you must pollinate the white flowers with a paint brush; otherwise there will be no fruits.

Sparmannia africana (African hemp or House lime)—these decorative bushy plants, with large, hairy, light green leaves and yellowish-white flower umbels, need a light airy place which is cool in winter. In the summer they need shade in the open air. Water and feed plentifully during the growing season.

Zantedeschia aethiopica (Arum or Calla lily)—the white sheath-like flowers with the yellow stamen in the middle only appear when after blooming in May/June, the plant has passed through a rest period, during which it is not watered and nearly all the leaves die off. In summer it is best in the open. It should be kept cool until December and from January on somewhat warmer. It should always be kept in a light to sunny spot.

Urn plant

Only a few plants can stand warm dry air

Aechmea fasciata (Urn plant)—a member of the great bromeliad family, with stiff, silver-grey, banded leaves which form a funnel round the thick spike which supports the little blue flower and the surrounding pink leaves. The plant blooms only once after which, with proper care, it will form offshoots and then slowly die off (after one to two years). The roots are used almost exclusively for holding the plant in position. The plant takes in water and nutrients through absorbent scales at the base of the leaf tube, the "urn". Pour soft water into the urn, give a weak feed during the summer months and moisten the root ball only slightly—no standing water!

Cissus antarctica (Kangaroo vine)—a creeper with light green, serrated leaves. In winter it likes a light but not too warm place (the higher the temperature, the greater the humidity and light it requires). It is very sensitive to wet and must therefore be watered with caution, particularly in winter. Shade from the full glare of the sun.

Clivia miniata—with ribbon-shaped, dark green leaves and vermilion flowers on a thick stem in spring. It can stand dry air and semi-shade but not standing water (give a lot of water at infrequent intervals). It is more likely to bloom if it is given a resting period from the autumn till the beginning

This is the situation we usually have in our living rooms in winter: a bright, well lit window-sill, a radiator underneath, and an almost even temperature of 65°F (18°C) and more. Protection from the fierce midday sun is important. Almost more important: you must make provision for humidity of the air. Then you can keep plants in places like these—those which are accustomed to high, even temperatures because of their tropical or sub-tropical places of origin.

Kangaroo vine

of January with little water and a low temperature (52°F or 12°C).

Cordyline (New Zealand cabbage tree)—a foliage plant with big leaves which grow to a point, dark green or red in colour, usually with a single stem and growing rather like a palm. It likes a bright but not sunny position. The varieties with brightly coloured leaves need a high degree of humidity.

Dipladenia bolivensis and *sanderii*—a plant which is partly bushy, partly climbing, with fresh green leaves and pinkish white flowers during the whole summer, and which needs a light position, but one shielded from the full sun, and a certain amount of humidity. If possible, the temperature in winter should not climb higher than 65°F (18°C), and is better at 60°F (15°C).

Dipladenia

Euphorbia pulcherrima (Poinsettia)—the plant with the brilliant red, occasionally pink or white too, bracts (the actual flowers are an insignificant yellow in the middle) is offered in flower shops before Christmas, usually as a single-stemmed, one-season plant which is thrown away after blooming. If you accustom it to your room temperature with some care (spray it frequently with lukewarm water and do not put in too warm a place to begin with, you can keep it for several years and bring it into bloom again. When it has finished flowering, trim off the tip, and the plant will branch out. Replant it in fresh soil in May and, during the summer, give it a light but not sunny position (out of doors), feed and water it generously, and bring it indoors to a well lit spot in September.

Poinsettia

Ficus elastica (Rubber plant)—one of the most rewarding house plants because of the way it stands up to normal room temperatures and lack of humidity. It is sensitive to standing water, particularly in winter (see page 17). Specimens which have grown too tall can be lopped in early spring or the top can be air-layered (see page 39); they will then grow side shoots. Wash the leaves frequently.

Equally tough, but even more decorative, are the Fiddle-leaved fig *(Ficus lyrata)* and the small-leaved Weeping fig *(Ficus benjamina)* which, with its gently drooping stems, resembles a little birch tree.

Fiddle-leaved fig

Hibiscus rosa-sinensis (Rose of China)—this is available with carmine pink double blooms, but also with single yellow flowers throughout the summer. It needs some humidity in winter and plenty of water and nutrients in summer. Cut back boldly to the old wood in late winter, and frequently prune the young shoots so that it breaks out and forms more flowers.

Wax flower

Hoya carnosa (Wax flower)—a climbing plant with shining green leaves, often flecked with silver, and soft pink, dark-centred flower umbels which look as if they were made of wax. Water infrequently, feed a little, and repot older plants only every two or three years. One important point: do not cut off the flower stalks when the flowers have finished blooming, for these form the new flowers for the coming year! They bloom better at lower winter temperatures (round about 54°F or 12°C). The related, non-climbing *Hoya bella* needs moister air.

Stephanotis floribunda (Clustered Wax flower, Madagascar jasmine)—a twining plant with leathery dark green leaves and fragrant star-shaped flowers clustering closely in umbels during the summer. It grows very vigorously and requires a trellis or canes to climb up. It likes some humidity in winter and the cooler it is the better it blooms (about 60°F or 15°C).

Madagascar jasmine

Foliage and flowers in the shade

Ampelopsis orientalis—a climbing plant with delicate, feathery five-lobed leaves, related to the Cissus. It needs semi-shade, a temperature between 40–60°F (10 and 15°C) and a certain degree of humidity.

Anthurium andreanum (Lakanthurium) and *scherzerianum* (Flamingo flower)—these are mainly offered as cut flowers, with dark green shining leaves and striking bright red, long-lasting flowers. The plant needs warmth, a relatively high humidity, a well aerated special compost mixed with plenty of peat, and it must have soft water. Keep well watered or, better still, soak it. It hates having "cold feet".

Begonia rex and many other kinds of bushy begonias—they are very decorative with their big leaves, hairy and patterned

Flamingo flower

There are many plants which are happy with a poorly lit position and even continue to grow and produce flowers there. But often you want the cheerful green of a plant for a dark corner in your room, in the hall or on the staircase or even for a window that opens on to a light-well. Besides the "indestructibles"—plants which are particularly adaptable—there are other plants, principally from forest regions, which like a shady position. Depending on whether they originated in a tropical or temperate zone, these plants need high temperatures (59–64°F or 15–18°C) or low ones (50–59°F or 10–15°C). The general rule is that the higher the temperature the greater the humidity should be too (right up to the very primitive forest plants which need 75% and more humidity, and which are therefore possible only in specially built, glass-enclosed window gardens and cases; see Beautiful but delicate, *page 60). Plants from temperate zones need extra light when the temperature is higher than they actually need.*

in green, red and silver-white or with a metallic shimmer, and with white or pink flower clusters in spring. Provided the air contains a certain amount of humidity, the plants can stand normal room temperatures (the warmer it is, the more light they need, but not sun).

Brunfelsia calycina (Franciscea)—little shrubs with leathery dark green leaves and mauve flowers, which except for a few winter months appear nearly the whole year through. It likes damp air and temperatures above 60°F (15°C). It needs frequent pruning. Repot in the spring into shallow pots.

Dieffenbachia picta and other varieties (Dumb cane)—a foliage plant with big leaves, decoratively sprinkled with white, yellow or silver grey. It needs a relatively high humidity, particularly in summer during the growing period, and in winter temperatures between 60–68°F (15–20°C). Keep it moist all the time and shelter it from draughts.

Dracaena draco and other varieties (Dragon plant)—foliage plants with big green or green-and-white striped tapering leaves and orange-yellow roots. The richly coloured ones need comparatively high temperatures and humidity: the green ones can stand dry air, provided their position is cool. Prune older plants to make them break out or air-layer new shoots in order to rejuvenate the plant (see page 39).

Dizygotheca elegantissima (False aralia)—a decorative foliage plant with dark green serrated fingerlike leaves. It likes isolation, temperatures in winter not dropping below 60°F (15°C) and humidity during the growing period, particularly when it is young. Spray it frequently!

Ferns—a genus of plants which has many forms, no flowers, and whose members all need little light but a high degree of humidity, particularly during the growing period in spring. The temperature requirements vary according to the area of origin. Those suitable for cool rooms in winter are: *Phyllitis scolopendrium* (Hart's Tongue fern) with undivided, smooth or corrugated fronds, *Pteris cretica* with multiple feathery curly fronds, very resistant and adaptable, and also *Cyrtomium falcatum* (or *Polystichum*); for relatively warm rooms: *Nephrolepis exaltata*, with light green feathery curled leaves which can develop into large bushes and put out runners, and *Platycerium bifurcatum* (Stag's Horn fern) with grey-green, characteristically lobed and branching leaves—it can take warm, dry air indoors relatively well and also a well-lit position, provided it is frequently sprayed and soaked together with the shieldlike leaves which rest on the roots. Those which can be grown only in a warm temperature and high humidity, and which therefore do best in enclosed window gardens or in glass cases: *Adiantum* (Maidenhair fern), with graceful pale green leaves (which are red in the growing season) on dark brown wiry stems, and *Asplenium nidus* (Bird's Nest fern) with shining undivided leaves, regularly arranged and funnel-shaped. All ferns need aerated soil which contains peat, with lime-free or soft water is possible, and they should only be fed a little. An exception is the Stag's Horn fern which in its natural habitat grows epiphytically on tree trunks (i.e. as a kind of parasite) and is best treated as a hanging plant in the house. Because of its shield-shaped bottom leaves it cannot be watered, but only dipped; to feed it you insert lumps of peat soaked in a weak solution of fertilizer (preferably made from dried cow manure) in between the shield leaves.

Hedera helix (Ivy)—a climbing or hanging plant with heart-shaped leaves, splotched with yellow or silver-grey. It loves temperatures above 60°F (15°C) in winter, and with increased warmth it needs higher humidity and a lighter position.

Leaf cacti—in contrast to the round or cylindrical forms of the spiny desert cacti, these are forest-dwellers which usually grow epiphytically on trees. They therefore need a semi-shaded place indoors, shielded from the sun and because of their soft, leaflike members they always need adequate moisture, both in the soil and in the air. A rest period in autumn, or right into winter with the summer-blooming varieties, with temperatures round 60°F (15°C) and limited watering, encourages flower formation. Once the buds have appeared, do not move or turn the plants, or they will drop their buds.

To this group belong the Orchid cactus, *Epiphyllum* (formerly *Phyllocactus*), which bears large brilliant flowers in summer, *Rhipsalis* with plump, drooping shoots, *Rhipsali-*

Franciscea

Dumb cane

Stag's Horn fern

57

Orchid Cactus

Selenicereus

Kentia

dopsis (previously *Epiphyllum*), the Christmas cactus (*Zygocactus*, previously *Epiphyllum*), the most famous kind with white, pink or red tassel flowers and broad, leaflike shoots, which blooms according to its variety between Christmas and Easter, and *Selenicereus* with giant flowers of great brilliance, which bloom only for one night in summer.

Palms—in moderately warm rooms (54–58°F or 12–14°C) with little light the following do well: *Chamaedorea elegans* and Kentia *(Howeia belmoreana* and *forsteriana)*; in cool rooms the Date palm *(Phoenix canariensis)*, *Chamaerops humilis* and *Trachycarpus fortunei*. The latter prefer in summer a semi-shaded position in the open. The Coconut palm *(Microcoelum weddelianum*, previously *Cocos weddeliana)* requires temperatures above 65°F (18°C), high humidity and the constant presence of water in the saucer under the pot. All palms react badly to hard water. They must be kept damp all the time but if they are kept in cool rooms in winter, they should be kept slightly dryer. Repot as little as possible and choose a deeper rather than a larger pot.

Philodendron—many varieties—a genus with many forms, mostly more or less climbing or at least needing a support, with dark green or reddish leaves, often decorated with light veins or spots. The types with coloured or velvety leaves need temperatures above 65°F (18°C) and high humidity; the green and smooth-leaved are less delicate. The climbing *Philodendron scandens* (Sweetheart vine) belongs to the hardiest group of house plants.

Pilea cadierei (Aluminium plant) and other varieties of Pilea—a bushy plant with beautiful leaves patterned with silver, partly creeping. It does best at temperatures between 53–60°F (12–15°C) in winter and can stand normal room humidity. Spray it a little during the growing period in spring. Old plants are not attractive, so make provision for successors by taking cuttings during the summer.

Rhododendron simsii and *obtusum* (Azalea)—these beautiful bushes, which are on sale in the florists' shops from Christmas to Easter and which bloom again and again, love a semi-shaded position, cool if possible (50–60°F or 10–15°C) and a certain amount of humidity (the warmer their position, the more humidity they need, and also the more light, but never direct sunshine). In higher temperatures (normally heated living rooms) they become one-season plants which are not worth cultivating once they have finished blooming. In other circumstances replant them, after flowering, in shallow bowls or pots with a special compost (azaleas hate lime), keep them cool in semi-shade once again, sinking the pots in the garden (with peat) in the summer in a semi-shaded spot, water regularly (only with rain or soft water); in autumn keep them a little dryer but never let them dry out completely.

Aluminium plant

Saintpaulia ionantha (African violet)—this produces its brilliant purple blossoms (white or pink too in some varieties) nearly the whole year through. It needs a normal room temperature and some humidity, but it should never be sprayed with cold water or it will develop unsightly spots on its leaves. Keep it evenly damp but not wet (sink the pot in peat) and never give it cold water. New plants can be raised without difficulty from leaf cuttings, provided the soil is warm enough (see page 38).

Scindapsus aureus—a climbing or hanging plant with heart-shaped leaves, flecked with yellow or silver grey. It loves temperatures round about 60°F (15°C) in winter. If it is kept at a higher temperature, it will need higher humidity and a lighter position.

African violet

Selaginella (Tropical moss)—various varieties—many-stemmed, feathery foliage plant which resembles moss or fern. It has bright green, yellow or white foliage. It does best in winter temperatures of 60°F (15°C) and in fresh, damp but not stagnant air. Dryness is as dangerous to it as standing water. Water with soft water, feed a little and sink the pot in peat if possible.

Streptocarpus hybridus (Cape primrose)—this plant, which is related to the gloxinia, has broad leaves similar to those of the primrose, and delicate trumpet-shaped flowers, often striped in a darker colour, of red, pink, white, blue and violet shades. It blooms from May to September and often throughout the entire winter. It needs some humidity, normal room temperatures and protection from direct sun and draughts. Water plentifully and do not allow to dry out.

Scindapsus aureus

Cape primrose

Caladium

The plants in this group attract us in the hot house or the florist's shop. We would like to have them in the house too. But they have very particular needs.

Vriesea splendens (Bromelia)—a variety of bromeliad with regularly spaced, stiff dark-brown handed, funnel-shaped leaves, and a flame-coloured flower head which lasts for several months and which towers above the plant like a sword. In winter it prefers temperatures over 62°F (16°C), some humidity and lime-free water (pour it into the leaf tubes too). When it has finished blooming, the plant forms offshoots which should not be removed. With good care it is often possible to bring these to blooming. The mother plant does not bloom again but slowly dies off.

Beautiful but delicate

Acalypha wilkesiana and *Acalypha hispida* (Red hot cat's tail, Chenille plant)—shrublike plants, the first with bright red nettle leaves and the other with long-lasting, shining red tasselled flower heads. They prefer, light, warm, humid positions.

Aeschynanthus in various varieties—a hanging plant with yellowish red-tongued flowers in summer. They like semi-shade, temperatures round 62°F (16°C) and high humidity. Never give them cold water. They will only bloom again if they can pass through a rest period of at least four weeks between October and January at temperatures between 50–59°F (10–15°C).

Caladium bicolor in several varieties—a tuber plant with large heart-shaped leaves splendidly patterned in white, green and pink. It needs temperatures between 68–73°F (20–25°C) and high humidity in the early part of the year when the leaves are sprouting. Later on both can be reduced a little. From August the leaves slowly shrivel: the tubers can be left in their pots, warm and dry, for the winter and then placed in fresh soil in February and carefully watered.

Codiaeum variegatum (Croton)—a shrub with vivid leaves patterned in red, yellow and green, very colourful but also very delicate: if it is brought indoors from the greenhouse without being hardened off first, the leaves will drop at once. It likes a temperature above 61°F (16°C), and very humid air, but it does not like standing in the sun.

60

Columnea gloriosa, kewensis and others—a trailing plant with more or less hanging stems and tiny, fleshy, partly hairy leaves and brilliant red "throat-shaped" flowers from January to May. They need temperatures round 65°F (18°C), high humidity and a light position without sun. In autumn they should have a rest period at a temperature from 50–60°F (10–15°C) if you want them to bloom again.

Crossandra infundibuliformis—a small pot plant with shining green leaves and bright red flowers which appear at the tips of the shoots from March to November. It likes semi-shade, a lightish position in winter, humid air and even temperatures round about 65–68°F (18–20°C). Young plants need frequent pruning so that they break out. Feed generously but only when the soil ball is damp.

Gardenia jasminoides (Cape jasmine)—a little shrub which slightly recalls the Camellia. It has shining green leaves and heavily scented, white blossoms from May to October. It appreciates a light but not sunny position and needs a high degree of humidity. It is sensitive to hard water and to chilling of its roots.

Maranta leuconeura (Ten Commandment plant or Prayer plant)—a foliage plant with large oval, partially translucent leaves, the size of one's hand, beautifully patterned with dark spots and light veins. It can only do well for a long period if it enjoys high temperatures and very humid air in a shady window garden.

Medinilla magnifica—a very decorative, large shrublike plant with heavy red flower clusters in early summer. It needs a light to semi-shaded position, even temperatures between 61–72°F (16–22°C) and a good deal of humidity. It is often difficult to get this plant to settle down, but later it grows rapidly. Tie up the stems as they cannot usually support the weight of the blossoms. Feed and water strongly in summer, but keep it dry in winter.

Orchidaceae (Orchids)—there are some members of this family of exotic plants with their varying shapes and strange flowers which can be kept in the house, even to some extent without a specially constructed window garden. However, if you want to bring them into bloom, you must adhere

You can really only keep them permanently in a specially built window garden or in a display case which is glassed off from the living room. If you cannot provide this for them, and yet you receive them as presents, you should enjoy them while they are beautiful, and then part with them without feeling that your green fingers have lost their touch.

Columnea

Ten Commandment or Prayer plant

Medinilla

very closely to the greatly differing requirements of the individual types as regards temperature, humidity, light, growth and rest periods. Anyone who wants to make a hobby out of orchid-growing should first of all study the specialist literature and should also be ready to sacrifice his or her spare time to this activity. Frequently, instead of a bunch of flowers, you may be given an orchid plant in flower, and then you will want to try to keep it as long as possible—if you are lucky, it may bloom for several weeks. All orchids need absolutely lime-free water, both for watering and spraying (be careful: water drops should not be allowed to stand on the flowers). A semi-shaded, draught-free spot which is not too warm is best. The following are relatively hardy and easy to keep in the house: *Coelogyne cristata* with white flowers, *Dendrobium nobile* with small mauve flower clusters, *Laelia anceps* with pinkish-red flower spikes, *Lycaste skinneri* with pink and white flowers, *Maxillaria picta* with yellow and brown striped flowers, *Odontoglossum grande* with yellowish-brown flowers and *Paphiopedilum insigne* of the Lady's Slipper orchid group.

Tillandsia lindeniana (Blue bromelia)— a bromeliad with a broad, spatulate vermilion flower head, on which individual brilliant blue flowers appear one after the other. It prefers semi-shade and needs warmth and humidity.

The "indestructibles"
Asparagus sprengerii (Asparagus)—a plant with long needle-shaped leaves about $\frac{1}{2}''$ (1 cm) long on fronds often a yard (1 metre) or so long. It is often used to provide greenery for bouquets. It is happy almost anywhere, in contrast to its relative *Asparagus plumosus* (Asparagus fern) which has flat, wide-spreading scented leaf fronds which are also used a great deal in floristry and which can only be kept in a greenhouse or a window garden. Water freely from spring to autumn and feed well, trimming off unsightly fronds.

Aspidistra elatior—this foliage plant with shining dark green palm-like leaves can stand simply anything except glaring sunshine and standing water in its pot. Repot very seldom and split old plants to obtain new ones in early summer.

Bilbergia nutans—a type of bromeliad with narrow, grass-like leaves with a nodding pink flower cluster. It can de-

Blue bromelia

velop into a large plant suitable for a tub. It stands dry air, warmth and semi-shade, but not sun. It responds to occasional spraying and watering with soft water.

Chlorophytum comosum (Spider plant)—green and white grass-like leaf rosettes from which numerous young plants grow on long yellow runners. These quickly develop roots (see page 38); old specimens become unsightly and should be pulled up as soon as the plant has finished growing.

Cissus

Cissus rhombifolia—a foliage plant with triple-lobed leaves which in many varieties have a purple shimmer. It must be fastened to a trellis or treated as a hanging plant. It prefers a semi-shaded position and it can still do well at some distance from a window. However, it does need more light in winter if it is in a warm room.

Cyperus alternifolius (Umbrella plant)—a marsh plant with long-stemmed leaf whorls which resemble a little palm. It grows happily in any position, provided it receives plenty of water all the time. In summer it is best placed in a water-filled pot hider but in winter, particularly when there is less light and temperatures are lower, it is best kept somewhat dryer. Divide old plants or raise new plants from leaf whorls which are cut off and placed upside down in a glass of water to root.

Fatshedera lizei (Climbing figleaf palm, Fat-headed Lizzie or Ivy tree)—a foliage plant with decorative five-fingered leaves which likes a semi-shaded spot in summer and a bright one in winter (the warmer it is, the lighter it should be, but no sun!).

Fatsia japonica (Figleaf palm or Japanese aralia)—a foliage plant with big-lobed leaves, shaped like hands (usually light green but there are also forms with variegated leaves striped with white), on thin stems. It is happiest in cool, shady rooms, but it can also stand higher temperatures, but in that case needs more light and humidity when the young leaves appear. Water freely in summer and feed with caution.

Ficus pumila (Creeping fig)—related to the Rubber plant, it has small round leaves and many trailing branches. It needs

Fortunately not all house plants are so fussy about their requirements in the way of temperature, light and humidity. There is a whole range which displays an astonishing adaptability. They flourish as well in cool as in warm places, in light and in shade; and they can also stand comparatively dry air in the house. Of course, they have their optimum conditions, but they do not give up the ghost if there is too little of one or the other. With their help (and that of the corresponding one-season plants) you can extend the range of possibilities for unfavourable positions, and the beginner can use them to try out her talents and test the suitability of particular places.

63

Figleaf palm

Swiss Cheese plant

Peperomia

to be fastened to a support or treated as a hanging plant. Protect it only from the direct sun.

Helxine soleirolii—this forms tight, light green cushions of little round leaves on delicate shoots. It needs a relatively large amount of water, even in winter if it is in a light position and is continuing to grow. In dark cool spots in winter it needs only a little water or it will suffer from rot. Be cautious in feeding it! Rinse the fertilizer solution away with fresh water so that the leaves are not burned. Cut back plants which have become unsightly or propagate and renew them by division.

Monstera deliciosa (Swiss Cheese plant)—this is often incorrectly called "Philodendron" (there are types of Philodendron which resemble it, but they only have leaves with fingers, not those with holes in them). It does well even at the back of the room, some distance from the window. Too much light harms it. Do not cut off the aerial roots. Water it freely in summer and keep it dryish in winter.

Peperomia—various kinds—a foliage plant suited to dark positions. It has leaves similar in shape to *Piper nigrum* and in various colours according to type.

Piper nigrum—a trailing or climbing foliage plant with pointed heart-shaped, green or variegated leaves. It is quite content with only a little light but it needs some humidity when the temperature is high.

Sansevieria trifasciata (Mother-in-law's tongue)—as it can stand warm dry air in the house without turning a hair, this foliage plant with its thick, stiff leaves, banded in grey and green or often even striped with yellow, has almost become the "Number 1 House Plant". There is only one thing it cannot bear: cool temperatures below 50°F (10°C) and too much humidity in winter. If it is kept in a light, warm spot, it will produce delicate clusters of greenish white star-shaped flowers which are exquisitely scented towards evening.

Tetrastigma voinierianum—a vigorously growing climber with three- to five-lobed leaves like the horse-chestnut. It is only suitable for large rooms for the stems often grow several yards (metres) in a year. Feed and water freely in summer. In winter keep it somewhat cooler if possible (60°F or 15°C) and in a drier atmosphere.

Tradescantia—many varieties—a hanging or trailing foliage plant which is often called "Wandering Jew" because of its rapid growth. It is available in green or reddish, white or silver-grey striped varieties. Better suited to semi-shaded rather than to sunny positions. Old plants become unsightly and so you should make sure at the right time that you have new plants ready through stem cuttings (see page 38).

Achimenes longiflora

Plants which flower for a few weeks only

Achimenes longiflora—the numerous single flowers, violet-blue but also often pink or white, have a calyx which is set at an oblique angle. They must be kept rather damp (never use cold water!) and need a light position, shielded from the sun. You can comparatively easily bring them into flower the following year: keep on watering them until October and then gradually let them dry off. Leave the small scaly tubers in the dry pot for the winter at a temperature of 50–54°F (10–12°C). In early spring place them, several at a time, in a shallow pot in fresh earth, force them at a temperature of 68–77°F (20–25°C) and high humidity, feeding them frequently.

Aphelandra squarrosa—a tropical plant with beautiful leaves, veined in silvery white, and brilliant yellow flowers which grow thickly on an upright flower spike (the blooms last for three to eight weeks); it is sold in flower in spring and summer. It likes semi-shade, warmth and high humidity, It is possible to keep it growing in a hot-house but it does not really pay.

Aphelandra squarrosa

Begonia Gloire de Lorraine (Winter-flowering begonia)—one of the winter-flowering begonias one can buy, with big clusters of little pink or white flowers. The flowers often last several weeks if the plant is gradually acclimatized to the room temperature (54–60°F or 12–15°C—at first) in a semi-shaded spot with some degree of humidity. Water freely and cut off dead blooms.

Bougainvillea—during blooming it can stand in a warm

Slipper flower

Amaryllis

Not all the plants which the nurseryman offers us are intended to share our houses for a long time. These one-season plants, which have already occasionally been mentioned, usually appear on the market at certain seasons of the year. You bring them home in full bloom like a bunch of flowers—usually they hardly cost any more—enjoy them so long as they are in flower and then part with them.

Under favourable circumstances and with painstaking care you can keep a few of them throughout the year in the house, but often the effort is not worth while for the next crop of flowers is rather meagre, and the plants do not look very attractive in the intervening period. Many too are simply exhausted after their first flowering.

How long you can continue to enjoy the splendour of a flowering plant depends not only on the type of plant but also on its position; and a little care is, of course, also necessary.

sunny spot. Water normally. It is possible to keep it (see page 50).

Calceolaria hybrida (Slipper flower, Slipper-wort)—on sale in bloom in spring or early summer. The yellow to brownish-red flowers last for several weeks, provided the plant is kept in a cool, shady spot. It needs a great deal of water and humid air. Protect it from draughts!

Chrysanthemum indicum—in the past only available in autumn, but nowadays it is on sale in bloom nearly the whole year through in many varieties. It likes a light, cool place and air which is not too humid. Water freely. It is not worth while trying to keep the plant for another season.

Cyclamen persicum (Sowbread)—in warm dark rooms this counts as a one-season plant only. Often the splendour of its flowers is over in a few hours because of the too sudden transition from a cool greenhouse and because of its journey through the cold winter air into an overheated room. If the plant can be hardened gradually (keep it in a cool spot first), the blooms will last for weeks, and in a cool light spot it will flower all year (see page 51).

Hippeastrum (Amaryllis)—the giant white, pink or red trumpet-shaped flowers grow three to four on a stem, between January and May according to variety. If the plant is kept fairly cool, the flowers will last two to three weeks. If you have sufficient room, you can try to bring it into bloom again: when it has finished flowering, feed it generously and water normally. Leave off watering in summer when the leaves gradually turn yellow. The bulb must then remain, warm and dry, in its pot for several months. Then it should be repotted with care and at first watered only slightly until the flower stem is about the length of your finger. If you water too early and too plentifully, the flowers will "stick" and only leaves will develop.

Kalanchoe blossfeldiana—once this was available only from January to March, but now you can find this plant chiefly in the summer and autumn too. It has thick fleshy leaves and orange-red, or yellow, flower clusters, varying from 6–20″ (15–50 cm) in height according to the type. It stands dry air well and the flowering period lasts several weeks at temperatures round 60°F (15°C) and with a light but not sunny position. Water it with care but do not let it dry out. Buy only plants in full bloom, as buds hardly ever open in the house.

Primulas—you can buy the following kinds in pots for your room—*Primula malacoides* (Fairy primula) with several tiers of pink to lilac flowers, the white, red, pink or blue flowered *Primula sinensis* (Chinese primula) whose leaves are covered closely with hairs, and *Primula obconica* which is likewise white, blue, pink or red. The latter arouses an allergic skin reaction in sensitive people, but recently varieties have been developed which no longer produce the substance which excites the allergy. Primulas bloom during the winter months and *Primula obconica* for almost the entire year. They keep going for months in a cool, semi-shaded spot (somewhat lighter in winter), provided they are regularly watered, with the softest water possible, and are occasionally given a weak feed of fertilizer. Cut off dead flower heads.

Senecio cruentus (Cineraria)—a plant with large leaves and compact clusters of small daisy-like flowers in many strong and brilliant colours—blue, white, pink, bronze, red or banded in two colours—which has become rare, because it does well only in a very light (not sunny!) position at temperatures round 50°F (10°C): then the flowers last for four to six weeks. Water freely and spray frequently on warm days. When it has finished blooming in the spring, the cineraria is not worth keeping.

Sinningia hybrida (Gloxinia)—you can buy this plant with its velvety bell-shaped flowers in red, pink, white and blue, and also striped and banded, in spring and summer in full bloom. With good care you can keep it blooming in the house until autumn. It needs a semi-shaded place, an atmosphere as humid as possible and plenty of water, but do not let the water stand in its pot and do not water or spray with cold water.

Kalanchoe

Primula

Cineraria

Balconies and Terraces

Inside the house plants are your own private affair; on the other hand, plants on a balcony are part of the exterior. They are observed not only by their owner but also by passers-by who draw their own conclusions from the appearance of the balcony, the choice of plants and their condition. The balcony is not only a source of pleasure to the occupant but also at the same time a kind of visiting card.

A painting tip: choose white, grey or brown shades, for they will show the plants off to their best advantage. All other colours tend to obtrude slightly.

Plant containers

Wood, treated with a preservative and painted on the outside, has served as a material for plant containers since great-grandmother's day. Today wood is still a favourite material for plant boxes and it does its job well. However, you must reproof and paint it at regular intervals, if it is not to rot after a few years. Many paints and preservatives for instance, creosote and tar products, are harmful to plants. You must inquire beforehand from a specialist shop or experiment with great caution, and it is best to leave the containers standing empty for some weeks after you have treated them. You should always empty wooden containers in the autumn and store them in a dry place during the winter. You don't have this bother with containers of asbestos cement, polyester and other plastics, polystyrene and earthenware. They are weather-resistant (though asbestos cement and earthenware are breakable and can be damaged by frost) and need no protective paint. In recent years there has been an increasing number of plant beds built or moulded into the fabric of the balcony.

Choose the largest possible containers

Like the plants inside the house, the flowers on the balcony must make do with a limited amount of space for their roots. Most plant boxes are 5″, occasionally 6″ (12 cm, or 14 cm) deep and only 6″ (15 cm) wide. This is very narrow, particularly when the thickness of the sides takes up about an inch (about 2–3 cm) in wooden or polystyrene containers. You can only plant a single row of plants in boxes like these and you must look after your flowers with particular care.

With potted heathers you can prolong the season on your balcony into the autumn.

68

All plants will flourish more luxuriantly in deeper, wider containers, and their care will be considerably simpler: the earth will not dry out so easily, you will not need to water so frequently, and the temperatures round the roots will be more stable. The greater volume of earth contains a greater supply of nourishment, and in subsequent feeding the danger of burning the roots with too high a concentration of salts is lessened. Finally, with deep containers you can all the more easily do without drainage holes. Instead of these you can arrange a drainage layer, about an inch (1–2 cm) deep, of sand, gravel or vermiculite on the floor of the container.

While the depth and width of balcony plant boxes should not be too restricted, the length is a different matter. Movable containers which are taken inside during the winter or which are moved about from time to time (when you want to change your planting scheme according to the season) should not be too long or they will be difficult to handle.

In strong sunshine the soil in small plant boxes which are painted in dark colours becomes very warm, and this is not good for most balcony plants. Remedies: paint the boxes in a light colour; drape trailing plants over the edge to shade the walls of the boxes.

Drainage

Holes for drainage are only absolutely necessary when the containers are so shallow that you cannot insert an adequate drainage layer, and when they are so placed that they can be affected by large quantities of water in a sudden downpour of rain.

Containers which do not have a drainage hole must, of course, be watered carefully and with feeling!

Anyone who lacks confidence can construct a water-level gauge with a piece of tube cut to the depth of the container and a piece of stick (on the same lines as the dipstick on a car; see page 33).

With containers which do have drainage holes you must make sure that the excess water runs away in a direction that will not cause trouble—balcony owners on the floor below or people walking underneath do not enjoy unexpected showers!

If the plant boxes have holes for water drainage, then you will also need some means of catching surplus water and carrying it away. Some boxes are supplied with matching trays which go underneath.

Watering

As plants in a balcony container are packed closely together but at the same time are meant to grow luxuriantly, and as the soil in the containers dries out more quickly because of the sun and wind than the flower bed in the garden, the containers need particularly careful and regular watering. If the soil dries out more than usual on a hot day, then it may be necessary to use your watering-can two or three times a day. The work is simpler if the containers are large (see above) and you use a peat potting medium instead of compost; this can absorb a greater quantity of water without becoming waterlogged (see page 22).

Potting media
The best thing for filling the containers is the standard compost you can buy ready-packed in bags, and the other commercially prepared potting composts or soil-less composts (see page 20). You can also ask your nurseryman for potting soil.

Compost from a compost heap which has not been properly managed or even plain garden earth is not recommended. These soils do not contain sufficient nutrients, they are not proof against waterlogging and they can bring with them disease organisms and parasites. Soil from a nursery and soil-less composts will have been sterilized.

Fertilizing
Although standard and soil-less composts already contain a certain amount of plant food, all plants in balcony containers should be regularly fed comparatively soon after being planted, if they are intended to grow quickly and to bloom plentifully. The initial nutrient content of the soil will be exhausted after four to six weeks, depending on the speed of growth. Then you must feed every eight to fourteen days, using for the sake of simplicity and safety one of the usual commercially prepared compound fertilizers in powder, water-soluble or liquid form, properly diluted (see page 23). Large but weak doses of fertilizer have a better and more even effect than more infrequent ones of a strong solution which, because of the small quantities, may cause slight burn damage to the base of the plant. You should never water the plants with a fertilizer solution when they are bone-dry (see page 25).

Renew the soil every year
It is false economy to try to use last year's earth again for the coming year, even if it has been freshened up with a few handfuls of peat and fertilizer. Summer flowers with their profusion of blooms take all they can out of the soil and also, during the course of the summer, deposits from watering and fertilizing, disease organisms and pests collect in the soil. Therefore you should renew the soil in your con-

If balcony plants are to bloom profusely for a long time, they need regular and plentiful rations of water and nutrients from the very beginning.

The oleander, one of the loveliest tub plants for the balcony, needs plenty of fertilizer.

tainers every year, whether you empty them in the winter or not.

Even with a permanent display of dwarf conifers and perennials you should try to remove the soil, at least, in part, provided it is not involved with the roots of the plants, and to replace it.

With spacious containers you can always put the plant in complete with its pot (provided, of course, that this is of porous clay) and fill the space left with peat or peat compost. This has the advantage that you can easily change the plants when they have finished blooming or have lost their charms for some other reason. This method is also recommended for arrangements in which dwarf conifers and annuals are mixed.

Regular removal of dead flowers

Tidying-up sessions are part of balcony plant care too. All dead flowers must be removed at once in order to prevent the plant from setting seed, for then the formation of flowers stops. Balcony plants should not form fruit but should flower for as many weeks as possible.

Pests and diseases

Pests and diseases are mainly caused by errors in management, by an unsuitable position or by unfavourable weather conditions. Healthy growing plants are hardly ever attacked by pests or diseases. The most convenient way of combating them is with a proprietary aerosol spray (there are sprays for insect attacks and combination sprays which help against fungal disease at the same time), with a powder or with a preparation which is used to make a solution which can be sprayed on (see page 42).

Viola cornuta is one of the long-lasting alpines. It blooms the whole summer through.

Nearly all the products for fighting against pest and disease attack are more or less poisonous. You should therefore use them with caution, following the instructions exactly, and should take care to keep them under lock and key.

Choosing the Right Plants

Obviously the same considerations apply to plants for the balcony as to plants for the home. The first question should not be "What do I want to have on my balcony?", but "What can I grow successfully on my balcony?"

Sun-loving pelargoniums will not produce a single flower on a north-facing balcony where hardly a ray of sun ever penetrates, but only leaves; and petunias hanging from a cornice on the sixteenth floor of a tower block will always be blown to pieces by the wind. Nature cannot be forced, only outwitted. Fortunately the choice is wide enough in every case.

Choice of colour

It is also wide enough for another point, which is often overlooked in making a choice, to be taken into consideration: the colours. A balcony planted in all the colours of the rainbow can look very pretty, but it does not go with every house. A planting scheme in one or two colours looks much more effective in many cases.

In carrying this out you must first think of the background. Red or brilliantly pink flowers do not have a good effect in front of a dark red or brown brick wall; yellow or blue stands out much better. The colours of shutters, window frames, blinds and garden furniture should also be taken into consideration when you make your choice, so that the flower colours do not clash with them.

Plants for a sunny balcony

Ageratum houstonianum is one of the most useful summer flowers. It is blue, with various shades from lavender and sky-blue to dark and violet tones. It grows, according to variety, only 6–12″ (15–30 cm) high and is best suited for brightly coloured mixed plantings. It flowers indefatigably until the frost, provided the dead flowers are regularly cut off. Feed moderately and keep damp. A place in the full sun

Flame nettle

is preferred. It stops flowering during continuously damp weather. Buy young plants from a nurseryman each year.

Coleus blumei (Flame nettle)—these are very pleasant balcony plants whose decorative value lies more in the foliage, gaily patterned in many colours, than in their blue-violet flowers. They also do well in the house and are best raised afresh each year from cuttings or seed (you can also obtain young plants from the nursery). You can bring them through the winter in a moderately warm, very light room, but old plants become straggly and unsightly. Prune young plants vigorously so that they become splendidly bushy. Water with soft water only, use a soil-less compost or mix a good deal of peat with the potting soil.

Dianthus caryophyllus with its blood-red scented flowers, hanging down in dense clusters, is extremely beautiful but unfortunately somewhat delicate. It comes down to finding the good quality plants, the ones which have been properly nurtured (in the trade you will find many varieties which resemble these but which are disappointing when you try to carry them on over to the next season) and to having the right spot for them—sunny, with a high degree of humidity, but protected from rain. They also need a loamy soil, and the best fertilizer for them is dried cow manure. Anyone who has a very bright, cool but frost-free place in which to put them for the winter can grow young plants in autumn from cuttings.

Heliotropium arborescens (Heliotrope)—because of its height (20–24″ or 50–60 cm), this plant is suitable only for places which are sheltered from the wind or for bowls which are standing on the ground. It likes a warm place in the full sun. Our grandmothers in their time treasured the sweet vanilla scent of the dark blue, many-headed flower clusters which appear from high summer right into the autumn. It has little effect at a distance and so it is best to mix it with other flowering plants in white, yellow and red. You buy the young plants at the nursery. It is not possible to keep the plants for a second season.

Lantana camara are, in their sub-tropical habitat, semi-bushy plants, rather like the pelargonium. You can, however, obtain them as small bushy plants in flower from the

All balcony plants often do even better in tubs and bowl-shaped containers. But there is also a whole range of typical tub plants which are too big for balcony boxes. You will find a choice on pages 86–7.

Cucurbita pepo, raised on your own balcony, decorates the house with its gay fruit, which stay on the plant for a long time, right into autumn (see page 82).

Dianthus carophyllus

73

Lantana camara

nursery. The flower heads are composed of many individual flowers set together and the colour in them gradually deepens from the bright centre to the darker outer rim. The range of shades goes from bright yellow to brownish-red or cream-pink-lilac. They need full sun and stand up to dryness comparatively well. Feed in moderation. It is possible to keep them through the winter and to take cuttings (as with pelargoniums). If you have a suitably light place for them to spend the winter in, Lantana can also be grown in tubs as standards.

Lobelia erinus is available in bush and trailing forms. They form beds of flowers in light and dark tones of blue of an unbelievable brilliance which can be increased even further by planting a few pure white examples in between the blue ones. Picking off individual dead flowers is impossible and so when the first flowering is over in midsummer, you should cut them back about an inch or so (2–4 cm) with the shears. Then you will have a second flowering in the autumn —as long as you provide for sufficient moisture and fertilizer.

Pelargoniums—often incorrectly called geraniums. There are two groups: the upright, more or less compactly growing *Pelargonium zonale*, with rough hairy leaves, decorated with a brown band, and numerous single or double flower heads in many shadings of white through pink to dark red; and the loosely growing, hanging (or fastened to a trellis) ivy-leafed pelargonium *(Pelargonium peltatum)* with flat, light green leaves and single or double flowers in white, red and lilac. The French geranium *(Pelargonium grandiflora)* with large flowers, marked in the centre with a dark blotch, is more suited for cultivation indoors and only does well in rare cases in the open in very protected, semi-shaded spots. Zonal and ivy-leafed pelargoniums can stand sun and semi-shade, the latter being somewhat susceptible to wind damage. Feed them frequently, do not keep them too damp and regularly break off dead flower heads. Pelargoniums are perennial, shrublike plants in their home areas in South Africa and the Mediterranean. You can keep them in balcony containers for several years in succession, provided a suitable place is available for storing them during the winter. The best place is a light, frost-free but cool room with a maximum temperature of 50–56°F (10–12°C). They should

Lobelia

74

be brought inside in autumn before the first frost, pruned back a little and watered only sufficiently to prevent the soil from drying out completely.

Before they begin to break out at the end of February or the beginning of March, you should take them out of their containers or pots, shake the old soil off and plant them in new potting compost or soil-less compost. If they are placed in a very light spot, then the temperature should slowly rise until the plants are brought out into the open again in the middle of May. Pelargoniums brought on in this way often flower first. Leaving them for the winter in a dark and probably too warm (centrally heated!) cellar seldom works and hardly produces a single flower to cheer you in the following year.

Elderly plants become unsightly and overgrown and it is better to replace them with new ones from the nursery or to raise new plants yourself from cuttings which are taken in August and placed in small pots with a mixture of sand and peat (see page 38). By the winter they should be small plants, bushy with plenty of stems (prune them frequently), and they should be placed in a cool spot.

Petunia hybrida—these are prolific flower-producers if they are placed in the full sun, but they also flourish in semi-shade. There are countless different varieties, upright and bushy, dwarf or hanging, with single, double or fringed blooms in brilliant shades of red and pink, in white, in blue, in striped versions too, and recently in yellow and vermilion as well. All petunias are easily damaged by wind, particularly the hanging varieties and those with large blooms. If they are not kept damp all the time and given plenty of fertilizer, they will soon disappoint you. You can achieve a profusion of blossom right until autumn by regularly picking off dead flowers and the occasional pruning. They are annuals and are therefore discarded in the autumn.

Salvia splendens provides the brightest red of all the balcony plants—a red that clashes with all the other shades of red! It makes a very decorative display with yellow, blue or, loveliest of all, white flowers. You buy the young plants at a nursery and must make sure that they always have sufficient moisture when the sun is shining. Cutting off the dead flowers and giving plenty of fertilizer will ensure the formation of new flowers right until the late autumn.

Geraniums (or pelargoniums) are available in many varieties, upright and trailing. They like the sun but will also bloom in semi-shaded positions.

Petunia

If you want to make a bright display on your balcony, then make sure that the red tones of geraniums and petunias do not clash. It is best to put only white and blue petunias with red geraniums.

Begonia semperflorens

Tuberous begonia

Tagetes (African and French marigolds), provided they are well fertilized and watered and regularly freed of dead flowers, produce their single or double, yellow or reddish brown or even flame-coloured flowers indefatigably from summer until the frosts begin. The nurserymen are experimenting with new strains, trying to get rid of the acrid smell of the leaves which many people find unpleasant.

Buy young plants from a nursery (or you can raise them from seed in the house or under glass comparatively easily). Throw them away in autumn. The only varieties which are really suitable for the balcony are the dwarf ones *(Tagetes patula nana)*; they are particularly attractive with blue flowers such as *Ageratum*. The tall ones with large double flowers *(Tagetes erecta)* reach a height of 28″ (70 cm) and more, and are therefore better suited for planting in the garden or in tubs.

Plants for a shady balcony

Begonia semperflorens—this plant with its almost unbelievable number of flowers is an annual. It is bought as a young plant from a nursery in May and thrown away at the end of the season during which it usually flowers non-stop. Colours: pink, red and white. They need more sun than the tuberous varieties and damp fertile earth. If they grow tall and straggly during the summer, you can simply prune them back a little. They will then break out afresh and bloom again after a short period.

Begonia tuberhybrida (tuberous begonias) even in light shade also produce a great many flowers in brilliant colours, in white, yellow, pink and red, according to variety, individual double giant flowers up to 4″ (10 cm) in diameter, or numerous small ones 1–2″ (3–5 cm) across. There are also trailing varieties of the small-flowered type *(Begonia multiflora)* but which also grow upright to a height of 10–20″ (25–50 cm).

They are easily damaged by wind because of the weight of their flowers and the fragility of their glassy transparent stems. They need fertile, moist, but well-drained soil (the tubers rot in wet conditions) and should be given liquid fertilizer at frequent intervals till August. After that you reduce the fertilizer and water somewhat, so that the tubers prepare for winter.

When the first night frosts threaten, take them up on a sunny day and let them dry off a while in a warm dry place in the sun, out in the open or in the house, until the stems can be loosened without force from the tubers. You should carefully clean the tubers of roots and clinging soil, lay them in a shallow box with dry peat and place them for the winter in the cellar. At the end of March you can force them by placing them in a light warm position and carefully moistening the peat. You can also put them individually into pots in soilless compost. The upper side of the tuber (it usually has a little hollow in the place where the stem was the year before) should only be thinly covered with peat. Only after the second week in May should they be planted out in the open once more.

Begonia multiflora

Campanula fragilis and *Campanula isophylla* (Star of Bethlehem) do not belong to the group of strikingly beautiful balcony plants which create their effect at a distance, but rather enchant at a closer view through the profusion of their graceful, soft blue or white, star-shaped flowers on delicate, light green stems. They need a light position, sheltered from the wind, and a certain amount of humidity. They cannot stand burning sun. The soil should contain lime (use standard potting composts, not peat) and should be fertilized only until the end of June. They are perennials and you can keep them through the winter if you have a light but very cool room. In August, when flowering has ended, you should cut them back and replant them in fresh soil in early spring. Use small pots and divide the plants. They are also very suitable for cool rooms.

Star of Bethlehem

You can also grow fuchsias in tubs as small standards. They need somewhere light but cool for the winter.

Fuchsia hybrida—these flowers are among the favourite flowering plants for shady balconies, but they too have little impact at a distance. The hanging bell-shaped flowers, often two-toned and sometimes double, in pink, red, white and violet, appear from April to October (fuchsias cultivated in the house often bloom almost the whole year through). They like fresh humid air, a shaded to semi-shaded position and aerated, slightly acid soil, containing humus (mix with plenty of peat or soil-less compost). Feed with a compound fertilizer from April to August, water freely and never let the soil ball dry out. You can keep them during the winter in a light room at a temperature of 53–59°F (12–15°C) (in this case they retain their foliage and must be watered regularly); or you can cut them back in autumn and then store them in a very cool dark cellar at a temperature of

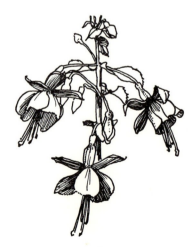

Fuchsia

A bird table contributes a great deal to the gaiety of your balcony in winter. It should, of course, be put into position before the severe cold sets in, at the latest by the end of November, so that the birds become accustomed to it and know, when food is short, where they will find something to eat. Twigs or small conifers will make it easier for them to land.

Hydrangea

Busy Lizzie

39°–43°F (4–6°C). They then lose their leaves and should only be watered very sparingly so that the soil ball does not dry out completely. Replant them in fresh earth in the early spring, put them in a warm light place, prune the new growth frequently, so that they become attractively bushy, and bring them out of doors after the second week in May. Older plants can grow into handsome shrubs if they are planted in tubs.

Hydrangea macrophylla (Hortensia)—these were originally tall, shrublike plants which one planted in sheltered places in the garden or kept in tubs. Nowadays you can buy dwarf, single-stemmed mini-varieties which form their pink, white or blue spherical flower clusters at a height of 6–8″ (15–20 cm). These plants make a rather short-lived but very decorative ornament for the shady balcony (you can replace them, when they have finished blooming in midsummer, with, say, chrysanthemums bought in flower). The cooler and damper their position, the longer the flowers will last (four to six weeks). Because of their large, soft leaves and big flower clusters, they need a great deal of water (water them at least twice a day in hot weather!) and protection from the wind. They do not stand up to cloudbursts very well.
Fertilizing is only necessary if you want to go on to grow them in a tub. Then you should cut them back when they have finished blooming, keep them somewhat dryer from August on and in autumn bring them into a very cool but frost-free room which should be dark. They will then lose their leaves. From April you can bring them out into the open again for further growth, but you must shield them from night frosts.

Impatiens walleriana, previously *Impatiens holstii* and *sultanii* (Busy Lizzie), known as a useful, indefatigably blooming pot plant for a sunless window sill, is also an industrious flower-producer in the open air too. It needs only plenty of moisture, humid air as well, if possible, and a strong dose of fertilizer solution every week. If the plants grow too tall, you can simply prune them and stick the shoots you have cut off into the earth or into water as cuttings. They will form roots within a few days. You can easily raise them yourself from seed or cuttings in the spring, but you can also buy them at a nursery as pot plants in full flower at very little cost. They cannot stand night frosts and you should therefore only put them out on the balcony after the second week in May.

Spring flowers for your balcony

All the balcony plants mentioned so far have come from warm zones and are therefore susceptible to frost damage. You can only plant them out when the danger of night frosts is finally over. As a rule, depending on the area, this is not before the middle to the end of May. But before this there are many lovely days which entice you to sit out in the sun on your balcony, and it is difficult to understand why the balcony containers should stand empty so long, when all around in the garden there are leaves and flowers. It is well worth-while lengthening the balcony's season by a spring planting.

A trip through your local market or a visit to a nursery in March will enable you to find a whole number of plants which even so early in the spring are already in bloom and which you can plant out in full flower, complete with the ball of earth from the pot. You may find *Bellis* (double daisy), *Myosotis alpestris* (forget-me-not), *Cheiranthus cheiri* (wallflower), various types of primula such as *Primula acaulis*, *Primula elatior* and *Primula denticulata*. All these plants flower for several weeks, provided you are careful to remove dead flowers at once, and to see that they always receive sufficient water.

One of the longest lasting of the spring flowering plants is our old friend *Viola tricolor* (pansy) which is sold in many colours and varieties. The *Hiemalis* variety can even be planted in balcony containers in autumn, provided the balcony is not too exposed to wind and frost. Isolated blossoms will open on mild winter days.

Of course, various flower bulbs will produce blooms in balcony containers, particularly hyacinths, crocuses and tulips: choose only the small early tulips and short-stemmed varieties: the tall ones do not have sufficient strength. But their cultivation is somewhat laborious: you cannot simply put the bulbs in the containers in autumn, but instead must embed them with their containers, or in pots, in earth in the garden (or store them in a large peat-lined box in a sheltered corner of the balcony or in a very cool room), and you should only bring them on to the open balcony when the tulips in the garden are showing flower.

In view of the short flowering period of all bulb flowers—

Primula acaulis

Pansies

Tulips

You can plant the bulbs of tulips, narcissi, hyacinths, crocuses and others in the garden, when they have finished flowering. They will often go on blooming there year after year (to ensure this you must continue to look after them until the leaves turn yellow of their own accord). You cannot use them any more for forcing.

White spruce

Picea abies nidiformis

Dwarf pine

it usually only lasts a few days—one might ask whether they are worth the outlay. Perhaps you might like to try the method out with a few pots which you can sink into the earth between other flowering plants (see above) and small conifers.

Balcony plants for autumn and winter

Usually the best you see on balconies in winter is an arrangement of cut branches of fir and pine. Young plants of the same trees are more attractive and longer lasting. You may be able to buy them not as pot plants from the nurseryman in the city but as young forest trees from a plantation (perhaps as the result of a country walk in late autumn), in which case they will cost little more than the branches. They should be embedded with their roots in the balcony containers and watered as necessary on frost-free days. In this way they will remain green and fresh throughout the winter and can, in certain circumstances, be planted in the garden in the spring. With the years, they will grow into stately trees.

If you have large, deep balcony boxes which are not too exposed to frost (tubs too are suitable for this), then it is worth-while looking out for dwarf conifers. Their shapes—shallow and spreading, globose, conical—and their differing types of needle in a rich blue or yellowish green bring variety to the winter balcony. These dwarfs are bought with a ball of soil round their roots and are not cheap, even if bought from a plantation. But they grow so slowly and are so modest in their requirements (they need only sufficient moisture, even in winter) that you can keep them for several years as a permanent display on your balcony. In spring during the period of fresh growth, they make a delightful background of fresh green for the first delicate flowers.

The best thing is to place them singly or in small groups and to keep putting new plants in between according to the season, first with spring and then with summer flowers. In the late autumn you can still obtain dwarf chrysanthemums or autumn-flowering heaths. Keep them in their pots and do not plant them out, and find out from the nurseryman whether they are of varieties which can stand mild frost at night. There are strains which are intended only for cool window sills and which become brown and ugly the moment the temperature falls below zero.

Types which are particularly suited for the balcony are the

dainty, sharply conical *Picea glauca* (White spruce), the nest-shaped *Picea abies nidiformis*, the blue-green *Picea abies glauca*, and of the false cypresses, which are often only thought of as hedging shrubs, the dwarf-growing forms such as *Chamaecyparis lawsoniana minima glauca* (Lawson's cypress), with blue-green foliage, the globe-shaped *Chamaecyparis filifera nana* with dark green threadlike shoots, *Chamaecyparis obtusa nana gracilis*, moss-green, with strangely twisted branches, and, for shady places, the dark green yew, *Taxus baccata repandens*. Some of the many creeping junipers are suitable for growing in containers on the balcony, *Juniperus sabina tamariscifolia*, for instance, but most of them grow rather rapidly, not so much in height as in breadth, and are therefore rather a nuisance on a balcony (but so much the lovelier in tubs on extensive terraces).

If you want to keep dwarf conifers in balcony boxes permanently, you must change the soil around them very carefully each spring, trying not to damage the roots. They react badly to hard water too: if you can water only with hard water, you must use water-softening tablets or soften the water with peat.

A Wall of Leaves and Flowers

Cup and Saucer vine

Humulus scandens

Nowhere are climbing plants so effective as on a narrow balcony: with a minimum of ground area you can have yards and yards of greenery and flowers growing, which make a refreshing summer display of foliage on a stone wall. Climbing plants need something to climb on, either a fixed trellis of wood, bamboo or plastic-covered iron rods (steel mesh is suitable too) or even spans of wire, nylon thread or tough string. Knots in the wire or string will ensure that the climbing plants will not suddenly break away when they have grown big and heavy. Some plants can hold on to the trellis by themselves by means of tendrils, leaves or shoots; others must be fastened in place. For both kinds it is important to install the support before you add the plants. If they do not find something to hold on to, and on which they can climb upwards, during the period of first growth, they will become stunted. Climbing plants too must be chosen according to the place they are to occupy; some like semi-shade, others the full glare of the sun. Nearly all climbers suffer if the wind is too strong.

The most attractive climbing plants

Cobaea scandens (Cup and Saucer vine)—this plant, which climbs of its own accord, with its large bell-shaped flowers which are at first greenish-white and later blue-violet, can, if it has enough fertile soil to draw on, cover several square yards (metres) with its green leafy screen. It prefers semi-shade and can stand some wind. It is difficult to raise yourself, and you will do better to buy young plants from a nursery in May.

Cucurbita pepo—with good fertilizing, plenty of water and an appropriate support, this plant will produce an impenetrable green wall and little fruits of many shapes in autumn. It can be sown in the middle of May directly into the containers; but it grows more vigorously and rapidly if it is raised indoors in peat pots from April on.

Morning glory

82

Hedera helix (Ivy) can form an evergreen wall on the balcony, but it does need a room container or tub and must be protected in winter from severe periods of frost, sharp winds and brilliant winter sunshine.

Humulus scandens forms a thick green wall of elegant feathery leaves. The flowers are insignificant. Sow at the beginning of April in peat pots indoors and plant out in the middle of May. It does not mind shade.

Ipomoea purpurea and *tricolor* (Morning glory)—these have fabulous bluish-white and pink flowers, but unfortunately they are somewhat delicate and need a good deal of warmth. The flowers are often only open for a couple of hours in the morning. Sow it at the end of April/beginning of May in the containers or raise it first in peat pots indoors. It needs ties or a fine mesh to climb on.

Lathyrus odoratus (Sweet pea)—this does best in full sun and humid air. It can be sown straight into the containers from the beginning of April till May. Place the peas singly at intervals of at least 2″ (5 cm) and later thin them out so that there is one every 4″ (10 cm). Give it plenty of fertilizer and water. It needs thin wire or string to climb on from the beginning.

Thunbergia alata (Black-eyed Susan)—from June till right into autumn it produces brilliant yellow flowers with a dark throat. It loves semi-shade and damp, fresh air. As it is easily damaged by wind, it does best on a veranda or even in a window. It must be grown from seed from March on in a warm room, and it is best to buy the young plants from a nursery in May.

Tropaeolum majus (Nasturtium)—there are many different varieties. Their shoots cannot cling of their own accord and so they must be tied on to the support. They can stand semi-shade but they bloom better in full sunshine. Do not give them earth which is too nutritious or fertilize them too much, or the leaves will hide the flowers! *Tropaeolum peregrinum*, with tiny yellow fringed flowers and very pretty heart-shaped leaves, even flourishes in the shade.

Sweet pea

Black-eyed Susan

Nasturtium

Plants for Tubs

Climbing figleaf palm or Ivy tree, really a house plant for cool rooms, can also be successfully placed in a tub on a balcony.

New styles of construction with wide terraces, roof gardens, projecting walls, large balconies and paved courtyards cry out for a comprehensive scheme of plant decoration. Tubs in all shapes and sizes are available, from the traditional wooden tub, through basins and urns of earthenware to the large containers made of asbestos cement and concrete.

They should not be too restricted in size as the plants need sufficient room inside for their roots. You can often observe that in bowls which have a very shallow extended rim the plants in the middle are the only ones that do well. Those round the edge cannot find enough soil for their roots. Rounded containers with almost upright sides are better for the plants, although they may not be so elegant to look at. The choice of plants that will flourish in a container increases with its size. As well as all the plants which are suited for balcony containers, you can also have the taller growing summer flowers which you can buy at a nursery or raise from seed yourself. For example, you will find the single dwarf dahlias, 20–24″ (50–60 cm) high, very attractive and rewarding, and the very decorative *Ricinus communis* (Castor Oil plant) with its giant hand-shaped divided leaves. But many summer flowers need a comparatively long "take-off" period. It is the middle of summer before they are in full bloom. If you don't want to wait so long, you will look for a permanent planting which can stay in the tub all the time. If the tub has sufficient depth and is not too exposed to the wind, you can keep nearly all hardy shrubs in it, from the dwarf conifers (see 'Balcony plants for autumn and winter', page 80) to the larger bushes and small trees. In choosing them, however, you should always take the advice of a specialist. Shrubs with tap roots which are accustomed to obtain their water and nourishment from the deeper layers of soil are always troublesome in tubs. You should not choose bushes which grow very quickly either. Better suited are slow growing dwarf forms such as *Acer japonicum* and *palmatum* (Japanese maples) or the curious *Rhus typhina* (Stag's Horn Sumach), and also the different kinds of Cotoneaster. Rhododendrons, hardy azaleas, *Calluna* (heather and ling) and *Erica carnea* (Winter Flowering heath) can be grown in tubs, provided you give them a lime-free soil mixed

Castor Oil plant

with plenty of peat and always use soft water. The following, all evergreens, are attractive in shady places; *Euonymus fortuneii*, *Prunus lauro cerasus* (Common laurel), *Ilex quifolium* (Common holly) and *Skimmia japonica*. These shrubs must also be watered in winter on frost-free days and need some protection from a drying east wind.

You can also keep roses in tubs, even climbers if you protect them from the frost in winter with an adequate packing of peat or straw. But all roses have deep roots and so they will not do as well in tubs as in the open ground. Dwarf or miniature roses which are only 8–12″ (20–30 cm) high are the best choice.

Hardy perennial bushes, which last as long as the shrubs but which do not make woody stems and branches, can also be grown in tubs. To the group of shrubs listed above must be added, in particular, those whose foliage forms decorative carpets of evergreen leaves, and perennial grasses. Finally you can arrange in stone troughs, in large bowls or on pieces of water-smoothed rock, miniature rockeries in which delicate alpine plants, varieties of *Saxifraga* (Rockfoil) or *Sempervivum* (Houseleek), well known for its ability to survive on poor soil, will flourish. Rockeries like this, if they are properly arranged, will need hardly any attention for years. You can also set up water and marsh gardens in appropriately sized bowls and troughs, with rushes, reed-mace, marsh marigolds, frogbit, flowering rush and even graceful little water lilies (there are varieties which are content with water only 4–6″ [10–15 cm] deep).

Finally there are still the classic tub plants which have served to decorate castle terraces and noble mansions for hundreds of years. They nearly all originated in sub-tropical zones and need a frost-free but bright and cool position in winter. This is probably why they went out of fashion for a while, just like the house plants of the first group (see page 50), the larger ones of which can be counted as tub plants. Who, besides the municipal Parks Department or a botanical garden, can provide them with an orangery as winter quarters? But journeys to the south have reawakened our love for these plants and perhaps the owner of a house or terrace here and there will consider whether he can squeeze in a small greenhouse for his tubs.

Single dwarf dahlias, only 20 inches (50 centimetres) high, are rewarding tub plants, provided they stand in a sunny spot and are plentifully watered and fed.

Dwarf rose

Indian mallow

African lily

Classic tub plants

Abutilon hybridum (Indian mallow)—a shrub with soft green or yellow-marbled leaves, similar to African Hemp or House Lime, with bell-shaped yellow, orange or reddish flowers which appear throughout the entire summer. If it has sufficient light, it can stand temperatures up to 59°F (15°C) in winter, but then it must be watered well, and in summer even more freely. Place it in a semi-shaded spot in summer and protect from sudden changes of temperature and draughts.

Agapanthus (African lily)—Plants with grassy, almost ever-green tufts of small ribbon-shaped leaves and brilliant blue spherical flower-heads containing up to a hundred long-lasting individual blooms. Keep very cool in winter, though out of the frost, place in the sun in summer, repot seldom, fertilize moderately, water freely in spring and summer but otherwise seldom.

Agave americana and other varieties—a succulent with a neatly arranged rosette of stiff-pointed leaves, which are hooped in blue-green or banded with yellow. The plants which date from earliest times bloom only once and then die off, but before this, however, they form offshoots. Agaves like poor sandy soil and should be only very sparingly watered.

Chrysanthemum frutescens (Marguerite)—the graceful marguerite with silver-grey, feathery leaves and little white and yellow daisy-flowers has lately also occasionally been sold as a balcony plant. Older plants form bushes, nearly a yard in height, which bloom from early summer into the autumn. Keep very cool in winter, cut back vigorously in the early spring, and cut off dead flowers. The best thing is to treat it in the same way as pelargoniums during the winter and to raise young plants in a similar fashion (see page 74).

Datura candida—a shrub from the thorn-apple family which can grow some two yards high in the space of three years. It has large elegant flower bells which are deliciously scented, particularly at night. Keep it through the winter at a temperature of 50–54°F (10–12°C), let it begin to grow at a warmer temperature from March on, and then it will bloom from April to November. Feed plentifully and water freely.

Replant it in early spring and in summer place it in a semi-shaded position, protected from the wind.

Nerium oleander (Oleander, Rose Bay)—a well-known shrub from the Mediterranean area with white, pink, red or yellow clusters of flowers which appear, according to the region, from April to August. In rainy summers the flowers often do not open at all and the buds will keep dormant during the winter and will open in due course next spring. Keep it in a cool light place during the winter, at 43–50°F (6–10°C), put it in a sunny spot in summer, water and fertilize freely. Take cuttings in early summer.

Plumbago capensis (Cape leadwort)—a half-climbing shrub which can also be grown as a pot plant. It has numerous sky-blue flower clusters from spring to autumn. Keep it at 35–50°F (3–10°C) during the winter and cut it back severely in the late winter. It likes fertile loamy soil.

Punica granatum—an evergreen shrub with leathery leaves and brilliant red flowers in spring and summer. In winter place in a very light, cool place, preferably at 45°F (6°C) and in summer keep in the full sun. Water freely in summer, moderately in winter, and do not over feed.

Datura candida

Oleander

Cape leadwort

Cut Flowers

Rose

Nasturtium

Cut flowers are intended for immediate use. But a bunch which droops within a few hours or even as soon as it is unwrapped looks dreary. It is worth while devoting a little trouble to looking after them so that you will enjoy them for a week or even longer.

Never forget the right way to cut
As soon as a flower or a twig is separated from the parent plant, the natural water supply is cut off and the water pressure (see 'turgidity', page 15) which keeps the leaves and flowers fresh and rigid is lowered because of evaporation; consequently the flowers wilt. You can limit evaporation to the minimum by wrapping the flowers up and keeping them cool. But one thing you cannot prevent: the entry of air through the cut into the sap channels of the stem. This air blocks the intake of water when the flowers are placed in water after a while, unless they are trimmed first.

You must therefore cut a further inch or so (2–4 cm) off the stems of all cut flowers before you place them in their vase. For this you can use a sharp pair of scissors or, even better, particularly for plants with thick or woody stems, a very sharp knife. The cut should be oblique and clean, and you should not crush the stem at all, for that will close the sap channels once again. Woody twigs, chrysanthemums and carnations can be broken (carnations at one of the knots in the stem). Hammering the stem, which is sometimes recommended, is unnecessary—if you do not do it properly, it closes the channels.

Fresh water and flower preservatives
Cut flowers should be given fresh clean water, but it should never be ice-cold—that would give them too much of a shock. The water should be room-temperature and so should that used when you change the water. This is certainly not necessary every day, but only when the water is stale and cloudy. You should rinse the stems thoroughly and cut the ends off again, and you should also wash the vase.

The clouding of the water is caused by bacteria and algae. These block the sap channels too and cause the flowers to wilt before they have properly bloomed. Various home

Chrysanthemums with large heads are very sensitive to jolts. If the stems are given a sudden jerk while they are being transported, all their flower petals will fall after a short while in the vase.

remedies have been suggested to prevent this, from copper pennies to aspirin tablets.

A more certain method is to use modern flower preservatives which have been available for some time now. These preservatives contain a disinfectant, which hinders the growth of bacteria and algae, and also sugar in a special form which is used to feed the flower. With the use of these preservatives the flowers last considerably longer, they keep their fresh colour and their perfume, the water does not need to be changed, merely topped up, and it no longer smells unpleasant (warning: the flowers will need more water than usual!).

These preservatives are particularly valuable for roses, carnations, chrysanthemums, freesias and all flowers which should not come into full bloom until they are in their vases.

Tulips continue to grow in their vases. As a result they often bend their stems in fantastic shapes. This can look very odd, if you do not re-arrange them during the daily water change (use flower preservative and only replenish the water that has been lost). If they droop too much, place them for several hours in the evening underneath a bright light, and then they will straighten out again.

Transport problems

Cut flowers must be protected as soon as possible against the effects of evaporation. They should therefore be well packed in paper for transport; it is even better if they are wrapped in plastic, sprayed with water perhaps beforehand (using a fine mist nozzle and water that is not ice-cold) and kept as cool as possible. Flowers which you buy early in the morning, or even the day before to give as a present, should not be wrapped; you should free the stems, cut the ends off and place them in a cool room, in the cellar if possible, in a little water (preferably containing preservative).

If you cut flowers in your own garden in the heat of noon (it is better to cut them dewy-fresh in the morning), you should arm yourself with a small bucket of water and put them into water straightaway.

If you want to bring a bunch of wild flowers back from an excursion, the best thing is to take a large plastic bag and a few paper handkerchiefs with you which you can dip in a stream and wrap round the ends of the stems. This method is useful too when you want to transport cut flowers for some distance. Then the best plan is to wrap the ends of the stems in damp cellulose wadding or moss with a waterproof outer covering of plastic or aluminium foil and then to envelope the whole bunch in plastic. In this condition fresh flowers will survive a journey of even twenty-four hours. If someone gives you a bunch of flowers, courtesy demands that you place them in a prominent position in your living room. Flowers which come in out of the cold of winter and

Freesias

For flower arrangements of all kinds there has recently become available in flower shops blocks of a feather-light, sponge-like plastic material (such as Oasis, Mosette, Florapak). You lay the blocks in water for a few minutes before you use them, until they are completely saturated and can then be cut or shaped as you choose. The flower stems are stuck into them (for soft-stemmed flowers you bore holes with a stick first) and the flowers behave just as if they were in a vase of water, provided you dampen the material from time to time. This material is extremely practical for complicated arrangements, for table decorations in shallow dishes and for flowers that you have to take on a long journey.

which are perhaps already beginning to wilt seldom survive such an abrupt change of temperature. They wilt before the eyes of guests and hostess. In cases like this it is better, and politer, to place the bouquet, with a brief explanation to the giver, first of all in a room which has a moderate temperature, perhaps even to give it a brief spray, and only after two hours to bring it into the living room, refreshed and adjusted to the temperature of your heating.

Reviving wilting flowers

As soon as you notice that the leaves are becoming limp or the flower heads are droppping, trim the stems once more, shortening them quite drastically if circumstances demand it; take off the big leaves, wrap the flowers in slightly dampened tissue paper and place them in deep water, if possible in a cool place. A bath in the bath tub or a large bowl often helps too, but many flowers do not react well to being thoroughly wetted.

Steam and candle flame

You can save roses which have begun to wilt by dipping the freshly cut ends of the stalks for about 30 seconds into boiling water and then placing them in luke-warm water. During this procedure the leaves and flowers should be protected by paper from the hot steam. Other flowers with soft, sappy stems too, particularly those with milky sap such as poppy, gerbera daisy, poinsettia and other euphorbias, should be turned upside down when the stalks have been trimmed for this hot-water treatment so that the sap does not run out.

The Japanese recommend yet another method: a brief singeing with a candle flame. It has the same effect: the sap coagulates and can no longer run out, but the sap channels remain open. The latter method is recommended for fresh flowers only, however, and not for refreshing older ones.

Tools and Supplies

While you have only a cyclamen or a couple of pots of primulas to look after and you throw them away when they have finished flowering, you will need hardly any tools for their care. Any old can will do for watering. However, as soon as you have more plants in the house (and there certainly will be more of them—you are given a plant which you do not want to lose for the sake of the giver, or you enjoy going from one flower shop to another), you will collect all sorts of accessories. And if you only have a couple of boxes on the balcony . . .

A good watering-can for house plants has a long thin spout, set low on the can, so that you can control the amount of water you are giving.

You need:

● a watering-can which will hold a fair amount of water so that you can always use water that has stood for a while—at least a quart to half a gallon (1–2 litres) for the house and 1 gallon (5 litres) for a large window garden or for the balcony. It should be light and easy to handle, having a long, low-set spout with only a small opening, so that you can direct the stream of water properly and administer the right amount (if the spout is set too high on the can and has too large an opening it is hard to avoid splashing). Plastic, galvanized iron or brass are all suitable materials.

● a plastic bowl or a small bucket that you can use for standing a plant in, for moistening peat and soil-less composts and for diluting insecticides and other chemicals; perhaps too you can use it for storing rain and melted snow.

● a small trowel for the plants on the balcony, for mixing earth and composts.

● one or two sharpened pieces of wood with which you can loosen the soil and the soil ball when you replant (or, more elegant, a set of indoor gardening tools in brass or stainless steel, with wood or bamboo handles, including an equally tiny rake).

● a small pair of sharp shears for the occasional pruning of your plants and for removing dead flowers and diseased twigs. The kind that grips the piece you have cut off is very practical.

● bast and wood or bamboo sticks, and plant supports of bamboo or plastic for climbing plants, for tying up and supporting plants.

The hand spray, worked by squeezing a rubber ball, is valuable for watering dishes and pots which have no space for watering with a can.

● a stock of peat, soil-less compost and standard potting composts (they are all available in handy plastic packs for home use) for repotting and filling troughs.

● gravel, crocks, vermiculite for making drainage layers.

● a compound fertilizer and possibly also special fertilizers for plants with particular requirements.

● water-softening tablets.

● plant chemicals (an insecticide and a fungicide or a combination of the two) in aerosols, or in powder or soluble form (and a suitable spray).

● a syringe for enveloping your plants with a fine mist of water in dry periods (it is also very useful for dampening clothes before you iron them!).

● a small hand spray with a rubber ball for swilling the dust off leaves and for watering pots and dishes which do not have a proper rim.

● a sponge or cloth for wiping leaves.

● a soft brush for dusting plants which do not like water.

● pots and dishes in various sizes as spares (soak new pots in water for twenty-four hours before you use them; clean old ones thoroughly and disinfect them).

● saucers that can go underneath pots, shallow trays and containers which can serve as pot holders.

● plastic bags.

and for your cut flowers:

● vases and bowls in many different sizes and materials.

● Oasis (or some other brand of plastic holding material), sphagnum moss and/or fine chicken wire.

● flower preservative.

● fine florist's wire in different thicknesses.

● pin holders in various sizes.

● smooth pebbles.

● a sharp knife for cutting ends off.

● pointed scissors for trimming and tidying.

● a deep pail, as narrow as possible, or a tall glass or pottery vase for freshening up tired flowers by standing them in water up to their necks.

A special work corner for flower care

For all these things you should try to keep one or two drawers in a chest free or a shelf in a store room, so that you do not have to search through the whole house when you need something.

It is even nicer if you can set up a special little working area somewhere, with a waterproof table top where you can work on your flowers without worrying about dirt or water splashes. The ideal arrangement is to have the whole place waterproof and easy to clean, where there is a tap and a drain nearby. But of course luxury of this kind can seldom be achieved unless you have a large house and can perhaps reserve part of the laundry for this purpose or install a hobby room.

Flower care is very easy if you have a special working area for it, with water laid on.

Index

Note: an asterisk denotes an illustration